TABLE MANNERS

JESSIE WARE   LENNIE WARE

Table Manners

THE COOKBOOK

EBURY
PRESS

Introduction

Jessie **On New Year's Day 2016, my good friend Jamie told me to start a podcast.**

A podcast fanatic, he said I was the nosiest person he knew and that I always managed to extract confessions out of people without having to work for it. I tried to think of the subjects that mattered most to me and combine them into a conversation. It took over a year to shape and start the podcast but in November 2017, my mum Lennie and I aired our first episode of *Table Manners*, our podcast about food, family and – much like all good dinner parties – wherever the conversation takes us. As a chronic oversharer and self-confessed 'nosy person', it seemed natural for me to start a podcast. What set it apart was roping my mum in, who had no idea what a podcast even was, asking that she host and cook dinner for each guest. Inspired by the raucous dinners of my Jewish upbringing, I wanted to a create a cosy, intimate environment where unfiltered chat could flourish, recorded over a home-cooked meal at my own or my mum's kitchen table.

My first love has always been food. I came out of the womb demanding milk, causing my mum's nipples to bleed from devouring her within minutes of being on this earth. My poor proud grandfather had to go into a pharmacy and ask for nipple guards to protect my mother's tired breasts and I don't think Mum has ever forgiven me for it. When I was nine months old, at a Spanish doctor's surgery with a chest infection, the doctor exclaimed: 'Muy gorda' ('really fat'). Things haven't changed. Mum says that my party trick was remembering which meal we had on the first night of every holiday. To be fair, it was almost always spaghetti bolognese, but it was unusual to have an adult's nostalgia for food at such an early age.

We grew up in south London, predominantly as a team of four: Mum, my elder sister Hannah, my little brother Alex and I. My father, John, is an investigative journalist and wafted in and out from whichever stakeout or current affairs investigation was dominating that month. But that was OK, even if most mealtimes were accompanied by a sibling slanging match or the chiming of 'But it's not fair!'. Mum would always have home-cooked meals for us after school, something she must have learnt from my Grandma, Gaga, who was one of the best cooks I knew. Dad would fill the downstairs with fried courgettes and the BBC's main current affairs programme *Newsnight*, a sound and smell that still feels melancholic yet reassuring.

I've never had any restraint when it comes to eating and my family still resent sharing a meal because it invariably ends up with me beating everyone to everything. I don't know why I've always been in such a hurry to eat my food, but it's never stopped the enjoyment. Ironically, we were the family that had a cupboard full of Wagon Wheels, Iced Gems and Monster Munch that were freely offered, but neither my siblings nor I were fussed about it. But when playmates would come over, that cupboard of sweet treasure would glow and drum like a heartbeat until they had demolished the lot.

My mum has always been the host with the most.

I was so impressed by how she would manage an evening meal for friends or acquaintances while still having what appeared to be all the time in the world to raise three children and work. Our house was a place of conversation and socialising, even with the frantic dashes to lay the table or finish a recipe with the clock running down. Although the guests would never see this, there would be clattering, theatrical shouts and groans about misplacing a pan or forgetting a key ingredient, but as the front door opened no one would have suspected any culinary jeopardy just moments before. She would have a dinner party nearly every week, with different strands of her and my dad's contrasting worlds, even adding a Sunday lunch into the equation for old family friends. There were always new dishes and old favourites, 'effortlessly' executed but always with huge consideration; from the array of nibbles and dips and music that filled you up before the main event, to the unbuttoning of your trousers to make room for the multiple desserts, our friends left in the early hours with bursting bellies and hearts. Even though I was never allowed to help with cooking the dishes, I was like a dog in a kitchen waiting for scraps, making sure I was on duty for serving up so that I could sneak a quick bite at the stove before our guests got to sample Mum's always exquisite cooking.

Rather than rebel and run away in my teens, I would confidently invite my friends over for a Friday-night dinner, along with their parents. My mum was brought up far more traditionally than me, so my Jewish heritage felt rather exotic, something to celebrate with others. With few Jewish friends, I was a rare breed in south London, so it made sense to welcome others into our incredibly relaxed yet ritualistic Friday-night world, full of chicken soup, chicken liver and an unruly kitchen. My sixteenth birthday was an innocent Sunday afternoon tea party. No stealthy shots of alcohol in tea cups, just tea, some cava, sandwiches and my brother's amazing cookies, which were the size and texture of all our teenage faces. My eighteenth was a marquee in the garden with Mum on canapés and vats of chilli (and some heavy kissing by the bins).

There was no eating in our bedrooms or in front of the telly: we would eat and drink together as family and friends, with Whitney Houston or Dusty Springfield playing in the background. And we had a great set-up: I would suggest or invite the guests – usually too many; Alex would set the table beautifully (usually done the night before) and make the pudding; Mum would do everything else. Hannah, not one for cooking, well, she would attend…

This has been an important Ware trait

to carry on with my own family, where we try to sit and eat together at any opportunity, even if my daughter shakes her head at a "mato' or declares she no longer likes spaghetti bolognese – but she already has an interest in cracking eggs, whisking creams and licking cake bowls. The kitchen is also where she is guaranteed to find me, and where we cook for friends. I have inherited my mother's obsession to *never* undercater, yet I haven't seemed to conquer her relaxed manner. I flit around the kitchen glugging wine and stirring pots with everyone ordering me to 'sit down'.

A meal can spark a memory so vividly: the pizza and garlic dip my now-husband ate on his own in his bedroom on our third date, with me looking on, desperate to have a slice but too petrified I would get it over my face or in my teeth and ruin the kiss. The comfort of cream on ice cream my mum offered me when I got my first period on a Welsh summer holiday. The Sunday roast that never got eaten as my parents sat in a car for hours shielding us from their imminent separation.

Table Manners came about through a desire to eat and talk with other people about their memories through food. It is so interesting to see how these memories can shoot off into such unexpected directions. Whether it's Raymond Blanc's memory of the perfect smell of the French countryside air while searching for frogs with his father, Joe Dempsie's happy upbringing on Findus Crispy Pancakes, Ed Sheeran's childhood Sunday meal being Campbell's Tomato Soup or Nigella Lawson revealing she was a fussy eater, we have learnt so much through our guests about all kinds of things. Who knew that I was such a stickler for timekeeping that I was quite happy to start a roast without a tardy Spice Girl? Which brings me on to Kiefer Sutherland's etiquette tip that you should, in fact, eat hot food as soon as it's served as opposed to waiting for others to start. Who would have thought that the writer of *Love Actually* and *Four Weddings and a Funeral*, Richard Curtis, would rhapsodise about the reality TV show *Love Island* being the greatest programme ever made? And just how many people have such an aversion to coriander, 'the devil's herb'?

It made complete sense to have my mum cook the meals. That's what she does so effortlessly. But I never expected people to share such similar obsessions as us, and what we naïvely started has turned into a community of salivating food gossips, a world of which I am extremely happy to be a part. I like to think that Mum and I have created an atmosphere where people feel comfortable about sharing (and oversharing), whether it's about food or what makes them who they are.

We have learnt a lot about cooking through the podcast: what is easy and what requires a little more preparation or at least a knowledge of your equipment before using it for the first time. Sometimes our best-laid plans have fallen by the wayside: the latkes for Loyle Carner that sizzled so loudly we couldn't hear him speak, the crème brûlée blowtorch that nearly set Mum on fire, or ordering an emergency takeaway when I had turned a promised succulent short rib into leather.

We have been travelling to the same little Greek island, Skopelos, since 1993. It has seen many a pivotal moment for the Wares: holiday romances, heartache, hangovers, sea urchin stings and urinated remedies, *Mamma Mia* films, engagements, weddings, the memories go on. So it felt right to include a few adored and borrowed Greek dishes along with other summer favourites.

This cookbook is a journal of some of my family's most pertinent and cherished food memories, along with friends' dishes, simple suggestions and hopefully exciting recipes for you to try at home. Throughout this book, we talk about special moments, souvenirs and domestic rituals for you to share and perhaps carry on with your loved ones.

My mum has always said we put the 'fun' in dysfunctional, which I guess is represented in this book. It's a dance through all the worlds of food we love, with recipes that will live on through sharing.

We hope you enjoy. Try and share a recipe or two with someone. Because that, to me, is the beauty of cooking.

Thank you. Love Jessie x

Lennie Jessie has always loved her food.

I remember when her little toes would wiggle with anticipation as soon as a plate of food approached her high chair. But then all our family loves food and entertaining, even though I am known to moan about the amount of work it involves and all my children say I have ruined many a Christmas by dropping constant reminders of how tired I am.

However, my whole family love parties and take pride in feeding large amounts of people with large amounts of food. The greatest accolade from any member of my family is, 'What a table!' as they admire a table groaning with large plates of delicious food. Everyone in the family can make a contribution and I hope my granddaughter is well on the way to attaining her hostess stripes.

My motto is never 'less is more'. I am always worried if there is not as much left over as people have already eaten – my motto has to be 'always have more than enough'.

I am close to all my children and they have always brought zillions of friends back home for dinner throughout their childhoods and as adults. We've always had lots of fun and I am so happy that I still see their friends and they enjoy coming over. Perhaps this is why Jessie asked me if I would like to help her do a podcast, based on the fun we had over large Friday-night dinners, mostly with her friends. There was already a huge number of converts to the virtues of chopped liver and chicken soup. So I agreed to cook while Jessie chatted to guests. Of course I could not remain in the background without making a vocal contribution, so I became part of the whole thing.

Jessie and I get on well despite the bickering and banter that you hear. She's a great cook and we complement each other, with my trusted recipes and her more modern and daring approach.

Enjoy this book. It's been such fun to make.

Love Lennie x

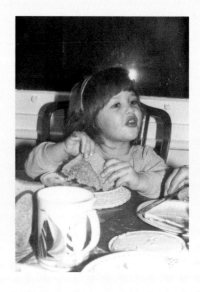

Effortless

Jessie **I am a self-confessed slap-dash cook.**

If there's a shortcut, I will gladly take it.
But I still love a good meal at any time of the day.

This chapter will hopefully help you out for a mid-week meal idea, a main to make quickly for family and friends, and sides that are so simple my toddler could make them. Among the recipes there are pitta chips and easy dips that are perfect with the Cosmo that Mum encourages everyone to drink; rustically pretty monkfish skewers that take no time to cook; drunken croutons; warming soups; sturdy sausage rolls; and plenty of helpful but delicious cooking cheats. These dishes have worked for us when we've had no time but still want to make an effort for our guests on the podcast.

At the core of this book is simple home cooking, with shortcuts, for real families with chaotic lives – the act of bringing everyone together to eat being the ultimate goal. So, here are a selection of quick, tasty, trustworthy dishes for any occasion where you don't want to slave over the stove.

Lennie **I always look for the effortless in cooking.** I worked, cared for my children and always enjoyed entertaining, so it helped to have good and easy recipes on hand. As I got older, I've learned how to make life easier for myself in the kitchen so that I can enjoy the fun and chat when I'm at the table. So, I either make stuff in advance or put effort into buying good-quality food that is simple to prepare and delicious when cooked. I recommend spending more on fish or meat from reliable shops, otherwise the effort goes into disguising cheaper cuts and cooking them more elaborately.

Yotam Ottolenghi has been an inspiration in terms of jazzing up vegetarian food and making it supremely delicious. My life goal is to learn to cook simple, tasty vegetarian dishes more easily, which Jessie seems to have mastered. And even though these recipes are effortless, they will work for all occasions, meaning you can relax and enjoy a cocktail.

Jessie's Granola

Jessie I have to make this indulgent but healthy delight every week, as my husband treats it like popcorn, and it brings the sweetest smell to a Monday morning. It's so versatile, you can use whatever nuts or dried fruits you prefer.

I switched from using sunflower oil after seeing that the wonderful chef and food writer Samin Nosrat uses olive oil and salt in her granola. Another brilliant suggestion came from a *Table Manners* listener, who suggested adding two whisked egg whites into the mixture to make it form delicious clumps.

Makes about 1kg

200g porridge oats
(gluten-free optional)

300g mixed nuts
(my favourites are flaked almonds, hazelnuts, brazil nuts and cashews)

150g mixed seeds
(such as sunflower, pumpkin or linseed)

1 tbsp ground cinnamon

2 egg whites

180ml olive oil

80ml maple syrup

pinch of salt

80g raw coconut flakes

150g raisins

OPTIONAL ADDITIONS
90g ready-to-eat dried apricots, dried apples, dried cranberries or dates, chopped

chia seeds

Preheat the oven to 170°C/150°C fan/gas 3.

Put the oats, nuts, seeds and cinnamon into a large mixing bowl and mix them all together.

Whisk the egg whites in a separate bowl for a few minutes until frothy.

Pour the olive oil and maple syrup into the bowl with the dry ingredients, add the egg whites and salt and mix thoroughly, ensuring all the dry ingredients have come into contact with the liquid ingredients. Spread the mixture evenly over a large baking sheet. Transfer to the oven and bake for 25 minutes.

Remove the sheet from the oven, add the coconut flakes to the mixture and give it a little a stir to ensure it's not sticking and the flakes are spread out. Turn the oven down to 150°C/130°C fan/gas 2 and return the granola to the oven for a further 15 minutes.

Turn the oven down to 120°C/100°C fan/gas ½ and bake for another 15 minutes to let it dry it out as much as possible.

Finally, scatter your raisins and other dried fruits and seeds, if using, into the mixture and give it a good stir. Turn the oven off, but return the granola to the oven and leave it until cold.

Store in an airtight jar for up to 2 weeks. Serve with yoghurt and fresh fruit or eat as a snack at any time of the day.

Hot Artichoke and Spinach Dip

Lennie The first time I tasted this was in LA, where it is often served with drinks before dinner. I ate so much of it that I struggled to eat dinner (only a little struggle, mind you). I've added spinach because I like it and because it gives a vibrant green colour. You can also add Tabasco and/or Worcestershire sauce for a bit of spice and tang.

400g tin artichoke hearts in water, drained

2 garlic cloves, crushed

120g mayonnaise

110g Parmesan, grated

handful of spinach

salt

Serves 8

Preheat the oven to 200°C/180°C fan/gas 6.

Put all the ingredients, except the salt, into a food processor and whizz until blended and smooth. Add a pinch of salt to taste.

Pour the dip into a shallow baking dish and bake for about 15 minutes, until hot all the way through.

Serve hot with Pitta Chips (page 28), plain pitta bread or tortilla chips.

Butter Bean Hummus

This can be made up to three days ahead: cover and chill until needed.

2 × 400g tins butter beans, rinsed and drained

2 large garlic cloves

4 tbsp tahini

6 tbsp fresh lemon juice

4 tbsp olive oil

1 tbsp ground cumin

salt and cayenne pepper

CRISPY SHALLOTS
3 tbsp sunflower or rapeseed oil

1 tbsp plain flour

2 shallots (or 1 small onion), thinly sliced

salt and pepper

Serves 8 as a starter or side

In a food processor, whizz together the butter beans, garlic, tahini, lemon juice, olive oil and cumin. Slowly add 3–4 tablespoons of water until you have the consistency you like. Season to taste with salt and a little cayenne pepper. Spoon into a bowl, cover and chill. Before serving, bring to room temperature; thin with a little more water if you like.

To make the crispy shallots, heat the oil in a pan over a medium–high heat. Season the flour with salt and black pepper, toss the shallots in the flour then add to the oil and fry, stirring occasionally, for about 10 minutes until deep golden and crisp. Drain on kitchen paper.

To serve, top the hummus with the crispy shallots and serve with Pitta Chips, (page 28), plain pitta bread or crudités.

Pitta Chips

Lennie **These are a great alternative to crisps and they can be flavoured and seasoned in so many ways. My son Alex started making these first and now we all make them when we're serving dips (they're best made on the day you want to serve them). So easy.**

6 white or wholemeal pitta breads, or a mix of both

2–3 tbsp olive oil or a flavoured oil such as chilli oil

sea salt flakes

OPTIONAL FLAVOURINGS
dukkah

sesame seeds

za'atar

Serves 8

Preheat the oven to 220°C/200°C fan/gas 7.

Split the pittas in half, then tear them up into pieces about the size of tortilla chips. Place on a large baking sheet, drizzle generously with the oil and sprinkle with sea salt and any additional flavourings. Spread evenly over the baking sheet so the pieces don't overlap.

Bake for 4–5 minutes. Keep an eye on them: after around 3 minutes they should be turning golden brown with a few crispy bits. Flip all of them over and return to the oven for another 4–5 minutes until the other side is golden brown.

Serve with Hot Artichoke and Spinach Dip (page 27), our Butter Bean Hummus (page 27) or indeed any hummus.

The Beloved Baked Potato

Jessie

My mother always thinks I haven't made enough of an effort when I serve up a baked potato, but I totally disagree. Why bother with a faffy hasselback (although, to be fair, I do enjoy them) when you can bung this in the oven for a couple of hours and there's no fuss? My friend Laura used to serve up the best lunch of baked potatoes with beans and Cheddar when we were writing songs together in her flat in West Norwood, south London. I looked forward to a rainy day of writing accompanied by this nostalgic meal. Even the Michelin-starred restaurant Brat in Shoreditch serves up a baked potato as one of their sides.

baking potatoes

olive oil or smoked rapeseed oil

sea salt flakes

butter, to serve

fillings (optional, see below)

OPTIONAL FILLINGS
2 tbsp Greek yoghurt mixed with 1 tsp Dijon mustard

cheese and grated raw carrot

baked beans (try them cold, trust me – it works!)

tuna mayonnaise: drain 1 tin of tuna and mix with a dollop of mayo, a little yoghurt, a good dash of red wine vinegar, salt and pepper and some chopped dill

Makes as many as you like

Preheat the oven to 200°C/180°C fan/gas 6.

Cut an 'X' into the top of each potato. Pour a generous amount of olive oil or smoked rapeseed oil into your hands and rub all over the potato, then rub with a generous amount of flaked sea salt.

Place on a baking sheet and bake for 2½ hours until the outside is crispy and the inside is soft. Serve with loads of butter and whatever filling you fancy.

Quick Lentil and Tomato Soup

Jessie Mum's always been great at soups. From her 'holy grail' Chicken Soup (see page 132) to the cabbage soup for that horrendous diet where you eat nothing else, she beats everyone I know when it comes to flavour.

Lennie My mum used to make this soup and it was always delicious. I've added cumin seeds as I've gone along and it tastes even better – I sometimes add fresh coriander, too. It's quick, easy and cheap to make.

3 tbsp olive oil

1 large onion,
finely chopped

3 carrots, finely chopped

3 celery sticks,
finely chopped

150g red lentils, rinsed
and drained

2 tsp cumin seeds

2 × 400g tins chopped
tomatoes

300ml boiling water

1 chicken stock cube

salt and pepper

Serves 4–5

Heat half of the olive oil in a large pan over a low–medium heat and fry the onion for 10–15 minutes until soft. Add the remaining olive oil, carrots and celery and sauté for a further 5 minutes until softened.

Stir in the lentils and cumin seeds, then add the tomatoes, water and stock cube, and season with salt and pepper. Bring to the boil, then simmer for 20 minutes or until the lentils are soft.

Use a hand blender to whizz the soup, leaving a few chunky bits for texture. If it is too thick, add a little more boiling water to loosen.

Benny's Drunken Croûton and Kale Salad

Jessie

This recipe stole the show when we invited Yotam Ottolenghi and his lovely husband Karl over for a 'relaxed' Sunday lunch. It's safe to say that the guest list for this lunch was larger than for any gig of mine – we were batting away people who threatened to attend in the hope of catching a glimpse of the King of Complicated, the Prince of the Pomegranate, the uniquely gifted chef extraordinaire.

Benny, my great friend and producer, was one of the fortunate few at the garden table. Benny is a food obsessive. I have had many memorable meals in New York and LA with Ben, including ones where he has cooked a feast for friends. I gave him his cherished copy of *Jerusalem*, so he jumped at the chance of making a salad to go with the hundreds of other dishes we had planned for months on end. We waited with baited breath to hear what Yotam would utter after a couple of mouthfuls of lunch; little did we know that he would talk about Benny's bloody croûtons over everything else. Crestfallen – and slightly jealous – we silently applauded Benny for his salad and decided that it seemed only right to include it in this book. This is a silent assassin of salads and has Yotam's seal of approval; need we say more?

200g kale, torn into large bite-size pieces

4 tbsp olive oil

6 tbsp grated Parmesan, plus extra to serve

juice of 1 lemon

DRUNKEN CROÛTONS
2 tbsp olive oil

75g butter

4 slices of sourdough bread, preferably a few days old, cut into rough 2cm chunks

120ml dry white wine

5 tbsp grated Parmesan

25–30g fresh parsley, chopped

salt and pepper

Serves 6

First, make the drunken croûtons. Heat the olive oil and half of the butter in a large frying pan over a medium–high heat. Add the bread chunks, ensuring that the crumb side (rather than the crust) is facing downwards. When they are brown on one side, about 3–4 minutes, flip them over, turn down the heat, and add the remaining butter and the wine to the pan (take care as it will go a little crazy in the pan). When the wine has evaporated and the croûtons are beautifully brown on the other side, toss in the Parmesan, parsley, salt and pepper and mix to combine. They won't be as rock hard as usual croûtons but should not be soggy. Transfer to a wire rack to cool down.

Meanwhile, put the kale in a large mixing bowl or serving bowl and add the olive oil, Parmesan and lemon juice. Using your hands, massage the dressing into the kale, removing any hard stalks as you go.

Add the croûtons to the kale salad, sprinkle with Parmesan and serve.

Onion Quiche

Jessie   We never thought a pop star would ask for a quiche, but this is what we heard Carly Rae Jepsen wanted. In fact, we'd got our wires crossed – it was that she made a mean quiche herself. So God bless a PR mix-up for Mum creating the most creamy and delicious quiche to ever touch our lips.

25g butter

500g onions, halved and finely sliced

plain flour, for dusting

500g shortcrust pastry

3 large eggs, beaten

300ml double cream

140g mature Cheddar, grated

100g Gruyère, grated

salt and pepper

Serves 8

Preheat the oven to 200°C/180°C fan/gas 6.

Melt the butter in a large pan, add the onions and gently cook for about 20 minutes until soft and turning golden. When they are nice and soft, turn off the heat.

While the onions are cooking, blind bake the pastry case. On a lightly floured work surface, roll out the pastry to about 3mm thick. Use it to line a 23cm loose-bottomed tart tin (about 3.5cm deep), leaving a little pastry hanging over the edge to allow for shrinkage. Prick the base all over with a fork, then line with a large circle of baking parchment (scrunch it up first, then open it out, so it's easier to mould into the case). Fill with baking beans or rice, then blind bake the pastry case for 20 minutes.

Carefully remove the parchment and beans, then bake for another 5–10 minutes until the pastry is cooked through and lightly golden.

Leave the pastry to cool for a few minutes before using a serrated knife to carefully cut off the excess pastry that is hanging over the edges.

Mix the onions with the eggs, cream and Cheddar and season to taste. Tip into the pastry case, then sprinkle over the Gruyère. Bake for about 25–30 minutes until golden brown on top.

Eat at room temperature with a nice salad. Our Slow-Roasted Tomatoes with Rocket and Green Beans (page 74) works well with this, too.

Marmite Carrot Soup

Jessie

Marmite sits high in my list of everlasting loves. A poached egg doesn't taste right without Marmite spread on buttery brown toast, and my offering to any late-night gathering in university halls was Marmite, crunchy peanut butter and grated Cheddar cheese on toast (tastes even better when stoned). I'll have it with marmalade, avocados, anything... it is the gift that keeps on giving.

My husband Sam introduced me to this soup with Marmite, a no-nonsense recipe passed down by his father Pete; it has saved many a miserable Saturday afternoon with a side of cheese and Marmite on toast. It's so simple and quick to make. Sam likes the soup quite thick, but if you like it thinner you can use more stock or even add some boiling water when you come to blend it.

Serves 6–8

20g butter

1 tbsp rapeseed oil
or olive oil

1 large white onion,
roughly chopped

1kg carrots, roughly chopped

1 potato, about 150g,
roughly cubed

handful of fresh sage leaves

1 tbsp Marmite

1.5–2 litres vegetable stock

2 tbsp cream or crème fraîche
(optional)

½ lemon

salt and pepper

Melt the butter in a large saucepan, add the oil and onion, cover with a lid and cook over a low–medium heat for about 10–15 minutes until soft and translucent. Add the carrots and potato and cook for 10 minutes, stirring occasionally, then add the sage and Marmite and stir to coat the vegetables. Add the vegetable stock, put the lid back on, and simmer for about 15 minutes until the carrots and potatoes are soft. Add a good pinch of salt and grinding of pepper.

Leave to cool slightly, then add the cream, if using, to give a more velvety texture.

Use a hand blender to whizz up the soup until smooth, then season to taste with a squeeze of lemon and some more pepper. Serve with Marmite and cheese on toast.

Primavera Risotto

Jessie   This is a springtime favourite and doesn't require much time or effort, just a little elbow grease for stirring the rice. And a generous glass of wine to drink while stirring. You can play around with any seasonal veg, but peas and asparagus are a must. I also think the crème fraîche adds a little more luxe to the dish, but of course my dear mother disagrees. You decide.

Lennie   I made up this recipe, inspired by vegetarian friends who cook wonderful dishes, including a version of this. It's nourishing, tasty and veg-based – who could ask for more, even as a carnivore?

25g butter

1 tbsp olive oil

1 large onion, finely chopped

1 celery stick, finely chopped

1.5 litres chicken or vegetable stock

500g risotto rice

300ml dry white wine

200g asparagus, woody ends removed, cut into 5cm lengths

150g frozen peas

70g frozen edamame or broad beans

180g baby spinach leaves

grated zest of 1 lemon

80g Parmesan, grated

1½–2 tbsp crème fraîche to serve (optional)

salt and pepper

Serves 4–5

Melt the butter with the olive oil in a large heavy-based pan over a low heat. Add the onion and celery and cook for 10–15 minutes until soft and translucent.

While the onions and celery are cooking, heat your stock.

Add the rice to the pan and stir to coat it in the oil, then add the wine and cook, stirring, until it is fully absorbed. Now, slowly add the hot stock in big splashes and keep stirring to ensure the rice doesn't stick. Add more stock whenever it has all been absorbed by the rice. After about 20 minutes, you will have added most of your stock. When you put your last splash in, add the asparagus, peas, beans and spinach and mix thoroughly. Continue to cook, stirring occasionally, until the asparagus is just tender.

Stir though the lemon zest, Parmesan, and salt and pepper to taste. For extra creaminess, stir through the crème fraîche. Serve immediately.

Toft Sausage Rolls

Jessie **Trying to solve a toddler lunch situation while attending a family member's wedding in the village of Toft in Lincolnshire, I tried the best sausage roll I've ever had. I robbed my daughter of her lunch because it was so moreish and delightful, and I felt no remorse. This is our version. If you prefer, you can cut them into smaller rolls for a bite-size snack.**

6 Lincolnshire sausages (about 400g)

325g sheet ready-rolled all-butter puff pastry

plain flour, for dusting

3 tbsp wholegrain mustard

90g mature Cheddar, grated

1 egg, beaten

1 tsp fennel seeds

Makes 6 large or 15 small

Preheat the oven to 200°C/180°C fan/gas 6. Line a large baking sheet with baking parchment.

Squeeze the sausagemeat from its skins into a bowl. Divide the mixture into 3 and shape to make 3 long sausages, each about 25cm long.

Unroll the pastry on a lightly floured work surface. Cut into 3 panels, each approximately 25 × 11cm. Spread 1 tablespoon of the mustard over each, leaving a 2cm border along one long edge of the pastry. Sprinkle the cheese over the mustard.

Lightly brush the border on each pastry panel with egg, lay the sausagemeat on the opposite side, then fold the pastry over the top. Use a fork to press the edges together to seal. Place on a chopping board and cut each large sausage roll in half, to make 6 sausage rolls, or into 5 to make 15 smaller rolls.

Place the sausage rolls on the lined baking sheet. Brush the tops with beaten egg and sprinkle with fennel seeds, then use a sharp knife to score the surface diagonally: this allows steam to escape. Bake for 20–25 minutes until the pastry is cooked and golden brown. Serve hot or cold.

Turkey Meatballs in Tomato Sauce

Jessie **These are light as a feather and seem to invite a confession, like when my dear friend the singer/songwriter Sam Smith explained they thought Mexico was in Spain while we fed these beauties to them.**

50g fresh white breadcrumbs

75ml whole milk

500g minced turkey thighs

2 garlic cloves, crushed
or finely grated

finely grated zest of 1 lemon

1 egg, beaten

40g pecorino or Parmesan
cheese, finely grated,
plus extra to serve

2 tsp finely chopped
fresh oregano,
or 1 tsp dried oregano

about ¼ nutmeg,
freshly grated

1 tsp fine salt

freshly ground black pepper

TOMATO SAUCE
2 tbsp olive oil

1 small onion, finely diced

2 garlic cloves, crushed

1 heaped tbsp tomato purée

1 tsp paprika (mild or hot)

2 × 400g tins chopped
tomatoes

1 large handful of basil
leaves

½–1 tsp caster sugar
(optional)

salt and pepper

Serves 4–6

First, make the tomato sauce. Heat the oil in a large sauté pan or shallow casserole over a medium heat. Add the onion and a good pinch of salt and gently fry for 5–10 minutes until softened. Add the garlic and fry for 2 minutes, then stir in the tomato purée and paprika and cook for another 2 minutes.

Tip in the tomatoes and chopped basil, then gently simmer for 20 minutes. Taste to check the seasoning, adding salt, pepper and a little sugar to balance the acidity of the tomatoes if needed.

Meanwhile, make the meatballs. Place the breadcrumbs in a large mixing bowl and pour over the milk. Add the turkey, garlic, lemon zest, egg, cheese, oregano, nutmeg, salt and a good grinding of black pepper. Using your hands, gently combine, taking care not to overmix. With wet hands, gently shape the mixture into about 20 small–medium meatballs (about the size of golf balls – roughly 40g each and 5cm in diameter).

Gently drop the meatballs into the simmering sauce, cover with a lid and simmer for 20 minutes, turning them after about 10 minutes and giving the pan a shake from time to time.

Remove the lid and simmer for another 5 minutes. Serve the meatballs with the basil leaves and a grating of pecorino or Parmesan.

Roasted Boursin Chicken and Leeks

Jessie

Table Manners now has an extended family that has embraced the Wares' dysfunctionality. Our cherished producer of the podcast, Alice, manages to edit Mum's and my nagging and madness into 'entertainment'. She lives up the road from me, has three beautiful daughters (my future babysitters) and a wonderful French husband, and she seems to love talking about recipes as much as I do. I'm in touch with my *Table Manners* family nearly as much as my own and the constant back and forth on menus means that every week someone will say 'What about this?' or 'You can't do that!'. Alice spent years in France, where she fell in love with Nicolas, Paris and the Basque Country, and has given me the following two absolutely delicious recipes inherited from her mother-in-law, as a reminder of her French halcyon days.

This is like a roasted version of chicken kiev. Put any vegetables you fancy in the roasting tin – I love to have leeks, celery and new potatoes. I don't save roast chicken for the weekend as it is so simple to do, making it easy to serve up a gorgeous meal.

1 large chicken, about 2kg, removed from the fridge 45 minutes before cooking to allow it to come to room temperature

150g pack of Boursin garlic and herb cream cheese

4 leeks, sliced in half lengthways

750g new potatoes, halved if large

5 celery sticks, trimmed and cut in half

2–3 tbsp olive oil

salt and pepper

Serves 4

Preheat the oven to 190°C/170°C fan/gas 5.

Using your fingers, gently ease the skin away from the chicken breast to create a pocket, taking care not to break the skin. Crumble half of the cream cheese and push it under the skin, massaging it so it covers the breast evenly. Put the remaining cream cheese into the chicken cavity.

Put the leeks in a large roasting tin and sit the chicken on top. Scatter the potatoes and celery around the chicken, drizzle with olive oil and season with salt and pepper. Roast for 1 hour 50 minutes, basting every 30 minutes. To check that the chicken is cooked, pierce the thickest part of one of the thighs with a skewer: the juices should run clear with no hint of pink.

Using a slotted spoon, transfer the vegetables to a plate and keep warm. Tip the chicken so that the melted cheese in the cavity runs out into the roasting tin, then set the chicken aside to rest for 10–15 minutes.

You should now have a roasting tin full of juices. Place the tin on the hob (or tip the juices into a pan if the tin is not hob-friendly) and cook over a medium heat for a few minutes, stirring often to create a creamy gravy. Serve the gravy with the chicken and vegetables.

Provençal Roast Chicken with Olive Tapenade

Jessie We made this at a lunch for fashion designer Sir Paul Smith and served it with green beans, a simple tomato and tarragon salad and Mum's Microwave Onion Rice (page 64). The tapenade oozes out to make a beautiful sauce to pour over the rice. The chicken can be served hot, warm or cold.

1 large chicken, about 2kg, removed from the fridge 45 minutes before cooking to allow it to come to room temperature

130g black olive tapenade

1 tbsp herbes de Provence

butter (optional)

3 garlic cloves, bashed

1 tbsp olive oil

salt and pepper

Serves 4–5

Preheat the oven to 190°C/170°C fan/gas 5.

Place your chicken in a large roasting tin. Using your fingers, gently ease the skin away from the chicken breast to create a pocket, taking care not to break the skin.

Tip half of the tapenade into a bowl (setting the other half aside), add the herbs and stir to combine. Spoon out about a quarter to a half of the tapenade-herb mix and push it under the skin of the chicken, massaging it so it covers the breast evenly. Don't worry if it's messy and oozes out. For extra indulgence, you could add a few small knobs of butter under the skin too.

Put the remaining tapenade-herb mix and the reserved tapenade into the cavity of the bird along with the bashed garlic cloves. Pour the olive oil over the chicken and season with a twist of salt and pepper.

Roast for 1 hour 50 minutes, basting every 30 minutes. To check that the chicken is cooked, pierce the thickest part of one of the thighs with a skewer: the juices should run clear with no hint of pink.

Remove from the oven and leave to rest for 10–15 minutes. Tip the chicken up so that any tapenade runs out into the roasting tin, then stir to combine the tapenade with the juices and serve as the gravy. Carve the chicken and serve on a large plate.

Beef Tagliata

Jessie Impressive in a ridiculously short time, this is a zesty, bright, summery take on the steak supper. This quick and easy meal is a real crowd-pleaser, although if you want to cook it for four or six guests, you'll need to do it in batches.

2 thick steaks (sirloin, ribeye or rump), 250–300g each

4 tbsp olive oil

3 garlic cloves, crushed

3 rosemary sprigs, roughly torn or leaves separated as wished

grated zest of 1 lemon, plus juice of 2 lemons

25g Parmesan, shaved

salt and pepper

Serves 2

Remove the steaks from the fridge at least 30 minutes before cooking and trim off all the fat.

Heat 1 tablespoon of the olive oil in a heavy-based frying pan over a high heat. Season the steaks, then fry for 5 minutes (for rare), turning once. Take the steaks out of the pan and set aside to rest on a plate.

Turn off the heat, then add to the pan the remaining 3 tablespoons of oil, the garlic, rosemary, lemon zest, salt and pepper. Mix well and leave to infuse for 3 minutes before adding the lemon juice and warming gently over a low heat for about 30 seconds.

Cut the steaks into slices about 1cm thick, return to the pan and briefly warm through in the aromatic sauce. Serve with shavings of Parmesan over the top and a side of baked or new potatoes and a salad. It also goes really well with chips or even potato dauphinoise.

Celeriac and Potato Gratin

A rich and fragrant alternative to dauphinoise potatoes.

25g unsalted butter, plus extra for greasing

400ml double cream

150ml milk

1 celeriac, peeled and thinly sliced

2 large potatoes, thinly sliced

80g Gruyère or Cheddar, grated

salt and pepper

Serves 8 as a side

Preheat the oven to 170°C/150°C fan/gas 3. Butter a large baking dish.

Warm the butter, cream and milk in a large pan over a low heat. Add the celeriac and potatoes and some salt and pepper and stir gently to ensure that the potato and celeriac are evenly distributed.

Tip into the baking dish and shake gently so the slices form overlapping layers. Top with grated cheese and bake for about 60–70 minutes until the celeriac is soft and the cheese is nicely browned.

Salt and Vinegar
Roast Potatoes

Jessie | Waiting for our baby son to arrive meant that my husband took a little pity on me and took me to a few lunches in our local area of east London. We tried out Jolene, the sister restaurant of Westerns Laundry and Primeur, and had fried eggs, *jamón* and potatoes. Only they weren't just potatoes… they were sweet-roasted with a subtle tang and tasted like the finest bag of salt and vinegar chips *ever*. I asked the waitress what was on them and she showed me the bottle of moscatel vinegar. I am sure you could use standard red wine vinegar, but now I have tried them this way, I have to use this kind. They go with roasts, cured meats, fish, everything!

1kg Maris Piper potatoes

80ml olive oil

70ml moscatel wine vinegar

salt and pepper

Serves 4 as a side

Preheat the oven to 200°C/180°C fan/gas 6.

Peel the potatoes and halve, or quarter if large. Put them in a large pan, add cold water to cover them and a pinch of salt. Bring to the boil, then turn off the heat, drain and put into a roasting tin.

Add the olive oil and 50ml of the vinegar and toss to ensure all the potatoes are coated. Season generously with salt and a little pepper, then roast for 50 minutes, giving the tin a shake halfway through.

After 50 minutes, add the remaining vinegar and cook for a further 10 minutes. Serve hot.

Parmesan and Spring Onion Mash

This is a simple side to go with any main dish. Don't go easy on the cheese!

1kg Maris Piper potatoes

100ml milk

40g butter

bunch of spring onions, thinly sliced

80g Parmesan, grated

salt and pepper

Serves 4–5 as a side

Peel the potatoes and cut into small pieces. Bring a large pan of salted water to the boil and put the potatoes in to cook over a medium heat for 15 minutes, or until tender but still holding their shape.

Drain the potatoes and put back into the pan along with the milk and butter, then mash until smooth. Add more milk if the mash is too stiff for your liking.

Add the spring onions and Parmesan and stir through. Season with salt and pepper to taste and serve hot.

Roasted Butternut Squash with Pink Peppercorns

Jessie Pink peppercorns are an unsung seasoning hero. Not only do they look pretty, they pack a delicate punch and jazz up a dish. I started using them after buying them in a supermarket in Greece. This simple roasted squash is a good side to have with a roast, or can be served cold in a salad.

1 tbsp pink peppercorns

1 large butternut squash, halved lengthways, seeds discarded

1½ tbsp olive oil

sea salt

Serves 4 as a side

Preheat the oven to 200°C/180°C fan/gas 6.

Roughly crush the pink peppercorns: use a pestle and mortar or wrap them in a clean tea towel (so they don't go flying all over the place) and bash them with a rolling pin.

Cut the squash into 1cm thick slices and place in a large baking tin (you may need 2 tins). Add the olive oil and crushed peppercorns and toss to coat the squash with the oil. Season with salt. Pop in the oven for 20–25 minutes, turning the slices after about 12 minutes, until the edges are starting to brown nicely and the squash is tender. If you are using 2 tins, switch them around halfway through so the squash browns evenly.

Serve hot, or leave to cool and store, covered, in the fridge for 1–2 days.

Asparagus with Anchovy Dressing

Lennie I tasted something like this at Skye Gyngell's magnificent restaurant Spring at Somerset House in London. This is my version. It goes so well with red meat, such as an onglet steak (see page 86) or a lamb dish, and is delicious hot or cold.

Anchovies are a great way to enhance flavour. They are wonderful with lamb and they also work well with potatoes in a gratin dish. Just don't tell anyone they are there and they will never know, even if they are anchovy-phobic like my son-in-law.

2 bunches of asparagus (about 500g), woody ends removed

salt

ANCHOVY DRESSING
8 anchovy fillets

1 garlic clove

10 capers

2 tsp red wine vinegar

120ml extra virgin olive oil

juice of 1 lemon

pinch of caster sugar

a few twists of black pepper

Serves 4 as a starter or side

To make the dressing, put all the ingredients in a bowl and whizz together using a hand blender.

Bring a large pan of salted water to the boil and put the asparagus in to cook for about 1½–3 minutes until just tender, then drain. If you are serving this cold, run the asparagus under a cold tap to preserve the vibrant green colour, then drain well.

Lay out the asparagus on a serving dish and drizzle about half the dressing over (any leftover dressing will keep in a sealed jar in the fridge for a few days). Alternatively, pour the dressing into a small bowl and serve as a dip.

Tip This works equally well with tenderstem broccoli – about 400g should be enough to serve 4.

Monkfish and Rosemary Skewers

Jessie   When we started this book, we asked all our friends what their favourite Lennie dish was. This little number was rediscovered after a 15-year hiatus. It's easy, gloriously aromatic and looks like Mum has turned into an avid forager (never). We like to serve this with Slow-Roasted Tomatoes with Rocket and Green Beans (page 74) and new potatoes.

Lennie   You will need some long sticks of rosemary foraged from a rosemary bush – yours or a neighbour's! I have never managed to grow rosemary but everyone else seems to. You may have to buy a living plant to make this, but rosemary will come in handy for many other recipes and your garden will look gorgeous.

600g monkfish, cleaned and skinned (ask the fishmonger to do this for you)

3 tbsp olive oil

grated zest and juice of 2 lemons

4–6 woody rosemary stalks, about 20cm long, most leaves removed

salt and pepper

Serves 4

Chop the monkfish into 4–5cm chunks. Mix the olive oil and lemon zest and juice in a bowl, add the fish and marinate in the fridge for a couple of hours.

Lift the fish out of the marinade and season with salt and pepper. Carefully thread the fish onto the rosemary stalks.

Preheat a griddle pan over a high heat. Cook the fish on the griddle for about 10 minutes, turning frequently, until just cooked. Serve immediately.

Pasta with Smoked Salmon, Vodka and Caviar

Lennie

A rather decadent and luxurious pasta dish that requires little effort. Rather than actual caviar, we use the lookalike black lumpfish roe you can find in most supermarkets.

400g linguine, farfalle or penne

200g crème fraîche

200g sliced smoked salmon, cut into strips

2 tbsp vodka

grated zest of 1 large lemon

2 tbsp chopped fresh dill

freshly ground black pepper

2 tsp lumpfish caviar, to serve

salt

Serves 4

Bring a large pan of salted water to the boil and put the pasta in to cook for 10 minutes until al dente.

Drain the pasta and return to the pan. Add all the remaining ingredients – except the caviar – and stir well until everything is warmed through.

Serve in bowls, grind over some black pepper and add half a teaspoon of caviar to each bowl. Alternatively, pile it all into a large serving bowl for your guests to serve themselves, dotting the caviar over the top.

Green Pesto Rice

Jessie Why reserve pesto only for pasta? Add it to rice and... Bob's your uncle, you have another way to satisfy a fusspot toddler. We use shop-bought pesto – saves hassle. We love to serve this with Marbella Chicken (page 100).

½ tsp salt

400g basmati rice

3–4 tbsp green pesto
(or more, if you like)

Serves 6 as a side

Wash the rice in several changes of water, until the water looks clear. Put 1 litre of fresh cold water into a pan, add the salt and bring to the boil. Add the rice and bring back to the boil, then reduce the heat, cover with a lid and simmer for about 10–15 minutes until the water has been absorbed and the rice is soft.

Add 3–4 generous tablespoons of pesto, stir into the rice and serve immediately.

Microwave Onion Rice

Jessie How did a microwave recipe get into our cookbook, I hear you cry? Because this is bloody good, easy and because we are not Julia Child or Delia. Mum's been making this rice forever and it just works. If you don't own a microwave, you can do this on the hob.

250g basmati rice (or mixed basmati and wild rice)

2 tbsp dried onions,
or ½ onion, finely chopped

1 tbsp sunflower oil

1 stock cube, preferably chicken, crumbled

½ tsp salt

Serves 4 as a side

Wash the rice in several changes of water, until the water looks clear. Put all the ingredients into a baking dish (about 1½–2 litres capacity) with a lid, or a microwaveable dish. Add about 450ml of cold water, enough to cover the rice.

Cover the dish and cook in the microwave on medium power (about 600W) for 10 minutes and then stir through. Put the dish back in the microwave and continue to cook on medium for another 10 minutes. Leave to stand for 5 minutes, then stir through and serve.

Courgette Bake

Lennie **I made this up when a friend gave me a load of courgettes from her allotment and everyone loved it. We serve this as a veg accompaniment to a roast.**

butter for greasing

1 small onion,
roughly chopped

4 courgettes (about 800g),
ends discarded

1 large egg

80g Cheddar, grated

½ tsp ground nutmeg

½ tsp salt

pepper, to taste

Serves 8 as a side

Preheat the oven to 200°C/180°C fan/gas 6. Butter a baking dish.

Put the onion and courgettes into a food processor and whizz until evenly chopped. Alternatively, if you don't have a food processor, just grate them. Add the egg, cheese, nutmeg and salt and pepper and whizz again or stir through.

Tip the mixture into the baking dish and bake for 45 minutes until browned on top. Serve hot.

A bit more effort

Jessie I will never forget our first ever live *Table Manners* booking at the Latitude festival, on the hottest day of the year.

We had decided to make a beetroot and gin-cured salmon for a man whose favourite meal was ketchup, the comedian and fellow podcaster Adam Buxton. Mum had been curing the salmon for 48 hours and then schlepped it to Suffolk, all sweaty and in need of some shade.

Now, as a musician, I have been doing festivals for years and what you grow to accept is the small ineffective fridge in your dressing room, a pack of warm beer and humming hummus. However, Lennie Ware played her rookie diva card and demanded that the space in the only working fridge be cleared out of booze to allow her gigantic salmon (find the actual recipe in the Chrismukkah chapter, page 198) to lay cooling. In hindsight, the two-day effort we put into this dish was wasted on Adam, who politely declined our offering, but is hopefully not wasted on you.

These recipes require some tender loving care, but there is nothing too strenuous. Some can be prepared the night before, like the Marbella Chicken; some taste even better the day after (though it didn't stop Ed Sheeran tucking in four times), like the Sausage and Bean Casserole; and some are best made minutes before serving. I remember not only actor Russell Tovey enjoying the Rare Onglet Steak but also his plus one, Rocky the French bulldog. Rocky cleverly managed to negotiate regular strips of steak being delivered under the table to stop his noisy paws rattling around the wooden floor while we recorded.

From slow cooking to overnight marinades, we hope you enjoy some of our favourite meals that we dish out to friends and loved ones and even pets.

Lennie Of course, I *always* make an effort – well, I always remind my family that I do!

But really, these recipes are not difficult and there is no need to spend hours in the kitchen. Sometimes, prepping the night before means you can really enjoy entertaining. When the children were at school and I was working, I would often make meals in the morning to be ready for the evening so we could all sit down together. It was so important to me.

Something I learnt far too late is to delegate! Get everyone to help: *don't* be a martyr who believes your only purpose in life is to be a 'balabusta' (boss of everything) and then get exhausted.

Smoked Mackerel Kedgeree

Jessie When I told my mother that I was making this for brunch for a *Table Manners* guest, the comedian and actress Cariad Lloyd, she rolled her eyes. However, I believe Mum went for seconds. The spicy onion mix can be cooked ahead of time and then it's a really quick dish to make that looks gorgeously colourful.

Serve with the Beetroot, Watercress and Hazelnut Salad (page 75) – it's an excellent combination with the mackerel.

50g unsalted butter

1 tbsp garam masala

1 tsp ground turmeric

2 cardamom pods, crushed

1 tsp coriander seeds

½ tsp yellow mustard seeds

5 dried curry leaves

1 large white onion, finely chopped

1 leek, finely sliced

2–3cm fresh root ginger, peeled and finely chopped, or 1 tsp ground ginger

small bunch of fresh coriander: stalks finely chopped, leaves roughly chopped

3 fresh or dried bay leaves

1½ tbsp curry powder

200g basmati rice

200g frozen peas

6 eggs

1 carrot, coarsely grated

250g smoked mackerel, skin discarded

grated zest and juice of 2 limes, plus extra lime wedges to serve (optional)

salt and pepper

Serves 6

Heat the butter in a large pan, add all the spices and curry leaves (but not the curry powder) and cook over a low heat for a couple of minutes. Add the onion and leek and cook for about 10 minutes until they are soft and golden.

Add the ginger, coriander stalks, bay leaves and curry powder and cook over a low–medium heat for 5–7 minutes. Season to taste, but don't over-season as the mackerel is salty.

Meanwhile, wash the rice in cold water to remove some of the starch; repeat 2–3 times until the water is less cloudy. Put the rice in a pan with 400ml cold salted water and bring to the boil, then reduce the heat, cover with a lid and simmer for 10–15 minutes until the water has been absorbed and the rice is soft. After about 10 minutes, add the peas to the pan so they cook with the rice. When the rice is cooked, remove the pan from the heat, cover the pan with a clean tea towel and let sit for 5 minutes.

Put the eggs into a pan of cold water, bring to the boil and simmer for 10 minutes, then put them into a bowl of cold water. When cool, peel and cut into halves or quarters.

Add the rice to the spiced onion mix, then add the grated carrot and flake in the mackerel along with the lime zest and juice. Stir thoroughly and serve with the eggs and chopped coriander leaves, with lime wedges, if you like.

Slow-Roasted Tomatoes
with Rocket and Green Beans

Jessie **A perfect addition to a summer spread, this also goes really well with the Savoury Cheesecake (page 79) or the Onion Quiche (page 35). Rather than drizzling the balsamic, I also like to use balsamic spray: two sprays per tomato.**

2–3 tbsp olive oil, plus extra
to serve

6–8 large tomatoes, halved

2 garlic cloves, finely slithered

1 tbsp capers

1 tbsp balsamic vinegar,
plus extra to serve

2 tbsp dried oregano or
chopped fresh oregano leaves

1 tbsp dried mint or thyme
or chopped fresh leaves

salt and pepper

TO SERVE
50g pine nuts

200g green beans

100g rocket

Serves 6–8

Preheat the oven to 140°C/120°C fan/gas 1.

Grease a baking sheet with ½ tablespoon of the olive oil. Arrange the tomatoes on the sheet and place a few slithers of garlic on each tomato along with 4 or 5 capers. Drizzle over the balsamic (or use a spray), then sprinkle with the herbs and the remaining olive oil. Season with salt and pepper and roast in the oven for 2½ hours.

Meanwhile, place the pine nuts in a dry frying pan and gently toast, shaking the pan occasionally, until lightly browned. Set aside.

Blanch the green beans in a pan of boiling salted water until al dente – 90 seconds should do the trick – and then plunge them into cold water. Drain and set aside.

Once the tomatoes are done, leave them to cool to room temperature. Arrange the rocket and green beans on a serving plate, add the tomatoes and scatter over the pine nuts. Drizzle over some good-quality olive oil and a little more balsamic.

See picture on the following page.

Beetroot, Watercress and Hazelnut Salad with Horseradish Dressing

This goes really well with oily fish. We make it for brunch as a side to our Smoked Mackerel Kedgeree (page 72). You could add some Puy lentils to make it more of a substantial salad.

80g hazelnuts, chopped

80g watercress

60g rocket

2–4 raw beetroots, peeled

HORSERADISH DRESSING
150g crème fraîche or sour cream

2 tbsp creamed horseradish from a jar

juice of ½ lemon, plus extra to serve

1 tbsp olive oil, plus extra to serve

salt and pepper

Serves 4–6 as a side

Place the chopped hazelnuts in a dry frying pan and gently toast until golden brown. Set aside.

Mix together the watercress and rocket and place on a serving plate. Grate the beetroots over the watercress and rocket.

To make the dressing, put the crème fraîche or sour cream in a bowl, add the creamed horseradish and squeeze in the lemon juice, then mix thoroughly. Stir in the olive oil, then season to taste.

Scatter the hazelnuts over the beetroot and add some generous spoonfuls of the dressing. Drizzle a little good-quality olive oil over the leaves and add a dash of lemon juice.

See picture on the following page.

Savoury Cheesecake

Lennie

This can be made really quickly, as we demonstrated on the podcast when our guest, broadcaster Amol Rajan, decided to tell us he was a veggie on the morning of recording. A cross between a quiche and a frittata, this is a versatile and lovely dish.

100g unsalted butter, plus extra for greasing

125g salted crackers (we use Tuc), crushed

1 tbsp finely grated Parmesan

1 white onion, roughly chopped

375g courgettes, grated

180g cream cheese

120g sour cream

1 tsp herbes de Provence

3 large eggs, beaten

200g Cheddar, grated

salt and pepper

Serves 8

Preheat the oven to 180°C/160°C fan/gas 4. Butter a 20cm loose-bottomed cake tin and line the base with baking parchment.

Melt three-quarters of the butter. Put the crushed crackers in a bowl, add the Parmesan and melted butter and mix thoroughly, then press into the base of the tin.

Heat the remaining butter in a large pan and fry the onion and courgettes for about 10–15 minutes until soft and most of the excess water from the courgette has evaporated.

Remove from the heat, stir in the cream cheese, sour cream and herbs, and season to taste. Add the eggs and the grated Cheddar, mix thoroughly and then tip the mixture into the tin, spreading it out evenly. Bake for 35–40 minutes until it feels firm.

Serve at room temperature.

Nora's Mushroom and Cashew Curry

Jessie

My friend offered me this spicy vegan curry as a natural labour induction when I was two weeks overdue with my son and despairing. Eventually he decided to turn up, and this perky dish was very welcome after weeks of newborn sleep-deprived nights. You can choose how hot you want to go, but I can confirm a curry does not start labour. Neither does having sex.

250g cashews

25g dried shiitake mushrooms

500ml vegetable stock, heated

1 tbsp sunflower oil

1 red onion, chopped

1 tsp garam masala

300g potatoes, peeled and chopped into 2cm chunks

1½ tbsp grated fresh root ginger

2 garlic cloves, chopped

handful of fresh coriander: stalks finely chopped, leaves roughly chopped

2 green chillies, seeded and chopped

½ tsp crushed chilli flakes (optional)

300g chestnut mushrooms, quartered

3 large tomatoes (about 300g), roughly chopped

salt and pepper

Serves 6–8

Preheat the oven to 200°C/180°C fan/gas 6.

Tip 75g of the cashews into a small roasting tin and roast for about 8 minutes until golden; set aside.

Soak the shiitake mushrooms in the hot vegetable stock for 30 minutes.

Meanwhile, heat the oil in a large pan over a medium heat and fry the onion for about 5 minutes until softened. Add the remaining cashews and fry for 5 minutes, then stir in the garam masala.

Toss the potatoes into the pan, along with the ginger, garlic, coriander stalks, chillies and chilli flakes, if using, and season with salt and pepper. Cook, stirring occasionally, for 5 minutes, then stir in the chestnut mushrooms and tomatoes.

Lift the shiitake mushrooms out of the vegetable stock (keep the stock) and roughly chop them. Stir into the pan along with the stock. Cover with a lid and gently simmer for 30 minutes, stirring regularly. Add a splash of water if it seems too thick.

To finish, stir through the toasted cashews, scatter over the coriander leaves and serve with rice and dairy-free yoghurt.

Aubergine and Puy Lentil Bolognese

Jessie

My mother, who rolls her eyes every time I offer a vegetarian alternative, had to text me after the Paloma Faith podcast to admit that 'the bolognese was delicious, darling'. I salute the brilliant vegetarian chef Anna Jones for putting dates in her recipe and blending half the lentils at the end for a perfect texture. This is inspired by Anna Jones' lentil ragu and is a tasty vegan alternative to spag bol.

4 tbsp olive oil

1 large red onion, thinly sliced

3 aubergines, cut into 2cm dice

1 white onion, finely chopped

1 celery stick, finely chopped

1 carrot, finely chopped

3 garlic cloves, crushed

1 tbsp tomato purée

¼ tsp ground allspice

½ tsp ground coriander

1 cinnamon stick

1 Medjool date, chopped

200g Puy lentils, well rinsed

400g tin chopped tomatoes

200ml red wine

400ml vegetable stock

1 tbsp freshly chopped oregano

salt and pepper

grated cheese (Parmesan or a vegan or vegetarian alternative)

Serves 6

Heat 3 tablespoons of the oil in a large frying pan over a medium–high heat and add the red onion with a good pinch of salt. Fry for 2–3 minutes until just softened, then add the aubergines and another pinch of salt. Fry for about 20 minutes, stirring regularly, until golden and caramelised. Tip the aubergine and onion out of the pan and set aside.

Add the remaining tablespoon of oil to the pan over a medium heat and gently fry the finely chopped onion, celery and carrot for about 5 minutes until softened. Add the garlic and fry for another couple of minutes, then add the tomato purée and spices and cook, stirring, for another minute.

Add the chopped date, lentils, tomatoes, wine, stock and oregano. Cover the pan and simmer gently for 25 minutes, then remove the lid and simmer for another 20 minutes to allow the excess liquid to evaporate. After this time, the lentils should be completely tender, but if not, add a splash of water and continue to simmer gently until they are.

Using a hand blender, pulse about half of the mixture: you can do this in the pan. This will thicken up the mixture while also leaving some chunkier bits. You may need to add a splash of water to loosen the bolognese. Stir in the reserved onion and aubergine, then taste and adjust the seasoning. Serve with pasta of your choice and grated cheese.

Sausage and Bean Casserole

Jessie We love a guest who doesn't hold back on seconds. Or thirds. But we applauded Ed Sheeran's gluttony when he went in for his fourth sausage helping. That's our kind of dinner guest. This is a hearty, no-nonsense dish that satisfies on a cold wintry night and keeps well, tasting even better the next day.

Lennie Use the best sausages you can find. Ed Sheeran couldn't resist! The sauce can be used as a basis for other stews too, not just the humble sausage.

3 tbsp olive oil

2 large onions, halved and thickly sliced

3 large garlic cloves, sliced

8 thick, well-seasoned pork sausages

glug of red wine

2 × 400g tins chopped tomatoes

3 tbsp wholegrain mustard

1 tsp dried rosemary

2 bay leaves

2 × 400g tins butter beans or haricot beans, drained and rinsed

salt and pepper

Serves 4

In a large casserole, heat 2 tablespoons of the olive oil over a low–medium heat and fry the onions for about 15 minutes until starting to colour. Add the garlic and cook for a further 3–4 minutes. Remove the onions and garlic and set aside.

Add the remaining olive oil to the casserole, turn up the heat and fry the sausages until nicely browned on all sides. Add the wine and let it bubble for 1–2 minutes.

Return the onions and garlic to the casserole along with the tomatoes, 2 tablespoons of mustard, the rosemary, bay leaves, salt and pepper; reduce the heat and simmer for about 5 minutes.

Add the beans to the casserole and gently simmer for 20–25 minutes until the sausages are fully cooked and much of the liquid has evaporated.

Stir in the remaining mustard and cook for another minute. Season to taste. Serve with mashed potatoes or crusty bread.

Rare Onglet Steak

Jessie   Onglet is the French name for hanger steak. It's perfectly tender
if cooked rare, otherwise it can get rather chewy and tough.
You could use an alternative cut like sirloin, but onglet is tastier
in our opinion. Buy it from a good butcher: the flavour will be better
and it is worth the money. But be brave and serve it very rare, with
Salsa Verde (page 111) and a green salad, and maybe sautéed potatoes,
potato dauphinoise or Celeriac and Potato Gratin (page 53).

This is not for the faint-hearted who do not like rare meat.
Actor Russell Tovey and Rocky the French bulldog loved it!

500g onglet steak

1–2 tbsp olive oil

salt and pepper

Serves 2–3

Remove the steak from the fridge about 30 minutes before cooking.
Pat the meat dry with kitchen paper, then rub the oil all over the meat
and generously season with salt and pepper on both sides.

Heat a griddle pan over a very high heat. Add the steak and cook for
3–4 minutes on each side.

Leave to rest on a warmed plate for about 20 minutes. It should be
eaten at room temperature.

Cut into 1cm thick slices and serve on a bed of salad along with some
salsa verde or a good strong mustard.

Dave's Devotional Thai Beef Salad

Jessie

Dave Okumu is a very important man in my life. He was the producer of my first record, *Devotion*, and has been my mentor in music over the years. I remember before our first 'blind date' writing session we emailed each other, gently getting to know one another. In one of those emails he reassured me by saying 'songwriting with a stranger is like purple bananas: it doesn't make sense'. We wrote about RnB, Sade, south London, how we took our tea, and which biscuits to bring to the session. Even though I hadn't met him yet, I was sure this was going to be a beautiful and lasting friendship. And it really was. He made those early steps in music feel effortless and fun. Making *Devotion* together was magical; we spent long summer days in his Lewisham flat working, confiding, eating – either treating ourselves to something from the local Italian deli or he would cook while listening to Grace Jones, Prince, and Wendy and Lisa. I was given an education by Mr Okumu, accompanied by sweet coffee with hot milk made on the hob and Prosecco at the end of the week. Whenever there was something profound to celebrate, it would rain. Dave said this was the heavens offering luck. This tradition has followed us ever since.

It felt only right to include a memory from that time in south-east London, and this is something Dave would rustle up for lunch.

Makes 10–12 lettuce cups

about 25g unsalted peanuts

100g basmati or jasmine rice

1 tbsp sesame oil

2 star anise

250g organic minced beef

2–3cm fresh root ginger, finely chopped or grated

1 garlic clove, finely chopped

1 tsp honey

2 Little Gem lettuce, leaves separated

1 carrot, finely sliced into matchsticks

1 red chilli, finely sliced

2 spring onions, finely sliced

15g fresh basil, leaves torn (use Thai holy basil if you can find it)

DRESSING

1 garlic clove, finely chopped

5cm fresh root ginger, finely chopped or grated

2 tsp fish sauce

2 tsp soy sauce

juice of 2 limes

Toast the peanuts in a dry frying pan over a medium heat, leave to cool and then crush with a pestle and mortar and set aside.

To make the dressing, bash the garlic and ginger in a pestle and mortar, then add the fish sauce, soy sauce and lime juice.

Cook the rice according to the packet instructions.

Meanwhile, heat the sesame oil in a large frying pan over a medium–high heat, add the star anise and the mince and stir with a wooden spoon to break up any lumps. Add the ginger, garlic and honey and stir-fry until the meat is cooked through and slightly crispy.

To assemble, take a lettuce leaf, add a mound of rice, a spoonful of beef, some carrot sticks, chilli and spring onions, then add a drizzle of dressing and garnish with the toasted peanuts and basil leaves.

Lamb Lebanese-Style

Lennie

This is probably my favourite dish to cook for a dinner party. The fragrance of the herbs and spices is wonderful, it's super easy and it goes with a variety of Middle Eastern vegetable side dishes. You'll need a butterflied leg of lamb (with the bone taken out) without too much fat on the outside. The only preparation is to marinate the lamb the night before you cook it. As there are no bones, it's quick to cook and easy to serve.

1 leg of lamb, butterflied, about 600g

2 tbsp olive oil

1½ tsp ground cumin

1½ tsp ground coriander

1½ tsp ground nutmeg

1½ tsp ground cinnamon

juice of 1 lemon

salt and pepper

TO SERVE (OPTIONAL)
handful of fresh coriander or mint leaves

Greek-style yoghurt, olive oil and cumin

Serves 4

Drizzle the lamb generously with the olive oil, season with salt and pepper, then rub in the cumin, coriander, nutmeg and cinnamon. Place in a large sealable plastic bag or a container with a tight-fitting lid, and leave in the fridge to marinate overnight.

Remove the lamb from the fridge at least 30 minutes before cooking. Preheat the oven to 220°C/200°C fan/gas 7.

Place the lamb in a roasting dish, skin-side up, and season with a little salt. Roast for 30 minutes, then remove from the oven and let rest for 10 minutes. The lamb will be tender, pink and delicious.

Slice and serve, sprinkled with the lemon juice. If you like, scatter with coriander or mint leaves and serve with Greek yoghurt drizzled with a little olive oil and sprinkled with cumin.

A BIT MORE EFFORT

Sticky Short Ribs

Jessie

This recipe is my mother putting forward the case that 'Mum knows best'. After a failed attempt at short ribs with singer George Ezra – resulting in me putting in a takeaway order at the local Turkish – Mum decided to make ribs for our next guest, TV presenter Dermot O'Leary, as a way to put me and my novice chef hat in our place. This recipe *does* work, with sticky splendour. Be prepared to suck those bones dry.

1 tbsp vegetable oil

1.5–1.8kg beef short ribs, trimmed of any fat and chopped into individual ribs (ask your butcher to do this)

2 onions, sliced

2 garlic cloves, crushed

1 heaped tbsp grated fresh root ginger

1 tsp fennel seeds

3 tbsp dark soy sauce

1–2 tbsp tomato ketchup

1 tbsp brown sugar

500ml fresh beef or chicken stock

juice of 1 lime

salt and pepper

Serves 4–6

Preheat the oven to 150°C/130°C fan/gas 2.

Heat the oil in a large flameproof casserole over a medium–high heat. Season the ribs and brown for 3–4 minutes on all sides: you may need to do this in batches, adding a little more oil. Lift the ribs out of the pan and set aside. Add the onions and garlic to the pan and cook for 5–10 minutes until soft, then add the ginger and fennel seeds and cook for 2 minutes. Add the soy sauce, tomato ketchup and sugar and cook for a further 3 minutes.

Tip in the stock, return the meat to the pan and bring to the boil. Cover and cook in the oven for 2 hours until the meat is soft and falling off the bone, then remove the lid and cook for a further 30 minutes.

The sauce should be rich and delicious: if it is a bit thin, lift out the meat using a slotted spoon and simmer the sauce on the hob for 10–15 minutes or until reduced and slightly sticky. Return the meat to the pan and leave to rest for 10 minutes.

Before serving, skim off any fat that has risen to the top of the sauce, then stir in the lime juice. Serve with mashed potatoes or rice.

Lamb with Pistachio Herb Crust

Jessie For me, a rack of lamb is the food of love.

My first Valentine's meal with my now husband was when we were 19. In fact, our first Valentine's Day fell two dates into our courtship a year earlier. It was a Friday night and I had already made plans months before with my friend Amber to go on a single girls' Valentine date in Brixton. How could I have known I would be invited on a *real* date with my future husband? So I promised both Amber and Sam I would see them and drank half a bottle of Amaretto for a little Dutch courage. As I slurred a nervous 'hello' to his parents, intoxicating their living room with lashings of sickly sweet perfume, I was a bag of nerves. Should I have got him a card or was that too much? Were we actually going to 'watch a film' in his bedroom? Would the Amaretto stay down on an empty stomach? But the thing that really threw me was, do I eat the barbecue chicken pizza (my favourite) with the garlic dip ordered by my suitor and risk food in my teeth and foul breath before our potential first kiss? I was so hungry but I weighed up all the risks and resisted the pizza, pretending I had already eaten. Sam shrugged and I looked on, longing for a slice yet hoping there was a kiss to come. After the film (and pizza) had finished, he drove me in his mum's car to Brixton and there we had our first kiss, all five seconds of it, as Amber interrupted us with the fifth call of the night.

Next year's Valentine's Day was our 'anniversary' so I rustled up a loving meal: a rack of lamb and home-made dauphinoise. The dish – albeit not much to look at – was a small declaration of love, so it made sense to try and woo the domestic goddess that is Nigella Lawson with a rack of lamb when she was a guest on the podcast. And it was perfect. Probably because my brother cooked it. But I will never forget Nigella sucking on those bones. A thing of beauty.

This dish is rather easy but looks incredibly fancy, perfect for a romance. Serve with coco de Paimpol or haricot beans and greens.

Lennie I first tasted coco de Paimpol beans at Skye Gyngell's restaurant Spring. The pods are a rather tired-looking mottled beige but the beans are pure white with a wonderful creamy texture. They're in season during summer and early autumn, but they are grown only in Brittany and naturally the French keep most of them. If they're not available, I use tinned white haricot beans to serve on the side with this beautiful rack of lamb.

Recipe on following page.

Lamb with Pistachio Herb Crust

2 racks of lamb,
French trimmed (fat removed
and bones cleaned – ask
your butcher to do this)

1 tbsp olive oil

3 garlic cloves, peeled

150g shelled pistachios

30g fresh flat-leaf parsley,
leaves only

30g fresh mint, leaves only

grated zest of 1 lemon

75g crustless bread, a day
or two old

2 tbsp Dijon mustard

salt and pepper

Serves 4

Preheat the oven to 200°C/180°C fan/gas 6.

Season the lamb. Heat a heavy-based frying pan over a medium–high heat, add the olive oil and brown the lamb for 2–3 minutes on all sides.

Whizz the garlic, pistachios, herbs, lemon zest and bread in a food processor until finely chopped.

Spread a tablespoon of mustard over each rack of lamb and coat in the herb mixture, pressing gently so that it sticks.

Roast for 15–20 minutes: 15 minutes will be very pink. Remove from the oven and leave to stand for 10 minutes before carving and serving.

Tip   If serving with tinned haricot beans, drain the beans and tip into a pan, adding a crushed garlic clove, a knob of butter, some chopped fresh parsley and half a chicken stock cube. Cook over a very low heat for about 20 minutes.

Butter-Poached Roast Potatoes

Jessie — Instagram can sometimes be good for the soul, especially when it comes to food. My friend once posted a night out, showing a butter-poached new potato with a little sour cream and caviar on the top. It looked equally ludicrous and divine. So I decided to try butter poaching, but adding something extra. I bought smoked rapeseed oil from a local farmer at the Bridport Food Festival and it has been the best addition to nearly everything. Serve these potatoes with simple pan-fried fish and salad or dress them up with sour cream and caviar.

50g butter
(salted or unsalted)

1kg new potatoes, halved

1.5 litres boiling water

6–8 bay leaves,
preferably fresh

1 lemon, cut in half

2–3 tbsp smoked rapeseed oil

sea salt flakes and pepper

Serves 4–6 as a side

Preheat the oven to 200°C/180°C fan/gas 6.

Melt the butter in a large pan, add the potatoes and toss in the butter for 5 minutes.

Pour in the boiling water, then add the bay leaves and squeeze in the lemon juice, along with the squeezed lemon halves. Cover with a lid and cook for 15 minutes.

Drain the potatoes, then place in a roasting tin along with the bay leaves and lemon halves. Add the smoked rapeseed oil and toss the potatoes until they are coated in oil. Sprinkle with salt and pepper. Roast for 40 minutes or until a good golden brown, giving them a stir after 15 minutes. Serve hot.

Marbella Chicken

Jessie The first time I tried this was at one of many Sunday afternoon gatherings with our friends the Sweeneys. The moment it touched my lips, it was love at first sight. It gives you everything: the sweet and the sharp, salivating taste buds and the depth of Mediterranean divinity. This dish was my first foray into confident entertaining (I think all my university friends tired of Marbella Chicken by the third year). It's a definite crowd-pleaser. I have even won over those irritating people who don't like sweet and sour flavours together with a plate of this. Everything can be prepped the night before, so you can be the host with the most and assume the title of an 'effortless cook'.

10 boneless skinless chicken breasts and thighs (4 breasts, 6 thighs), cut into large chunks (also see tip)

8 garlic cloves, finely chopped

2 tbsp dried oregano or chopped fresh oregano leaves

small bunch of fresh basil, leaves chopped

5 bay leaves

4 tbsp red wine vinegar

4 tbsp olive oil

2½ tbsp capers

about 20 green olives, pitted

10 ready-to-eat dried apricots, cut in half

10 no-soak prunes, cut in half

2 tbsp brown sugar

generous handful of red seedless grapes (optional)

250ml dry white wine

salt and pepper

Serves 5

Put the chicken into a large sealable plastic bag or a container with a tight-fitting lid, together with the garlic, herbs, vinegar, olive oil, capers, olives, apricots and prunes. Leave in the fridge to marinate overnight.

Preheat the oven to 200°C/180°C fan/gas 6.

Tip the chicken and its marinade into a roasting tin. Sprinkle over the brown sugar and add the grapes, if using. Pour the white wine around the chicken mixture and bake for 50 minutes.

Taste and adjust the seasoning. Leave to stand for 5–10 minutes before serving. Serve with rice: we like this with Green Pesto Rice (page 64).

Tip   You can use all thighs, which are more moist, or all breast pieces – in which case cook for a slightly shorter time to avoid dryness. Alternatively, use only skin-on bone-in thighs, which may need a slightly longer cooking time.

Kitty's Buffalo Wings

Jessie

Kitty is a nice Jewish girl who is obsessed with chicken wings and knows everywhere in London that serves them. You can find her at wing conventions (there is such a thing) or sitting on her own at her local pub enjoying a plate of them. She even hosts chicken parties, so this recipe has been absolutely perfected! I was never bothered about a wing – I felt they were the least satisfying part of the chicken (too much effort and mess) – but at our best mate's hen do, we were put in charge of the meals and I became sous chef to the wing wonder woman and now I am converted.

12 free-range chicken wings, about 1.2kg (also see tip)

100g plain flour

1 tsp paprika, preferably hot smoked paprika

6 celery sticks, halved lengthways and cut into 5cm sticks, to serve

salt and pepper

BUFFALO SAUCE
354ml bottle Frank's RedHot Original Cayenne Pepper Sauce

125g unsalted butter

5 tbsp honey

BLUE CHEESE DIP
75g Stilton, crumbled

100g sour cream

1½ tbsp white wine vinegar

truffle oil (optional)

Serves 6

Pat the chicken dry with kitchen paper. Fill a plastic bag (without holes) with the flour, paprika, salt and pepper. Chuck all the chicken in the bag and shake it about for 30 seconds until all the chicken is coated. Line up the chicken on a tray and leave in the fridge, uncovered, for 8 hours or overnight. The longer you leave them the crispier they'll be.

Preheat the oven to 180°C/160°C fan/gas 4 and line a baking sheet with greaseproof paper. Arrange the chicken wings on the baking sheet and bake for 30–45 minutes until just turning golden, then crank the oven up to 230°C/210°C fan/gas 8, turn the wings over, and cook for another 20–30 minutes. They're done when they're medium brown all over with little crispy bubbles.

While the wings are cooking, make the blue cheese dip. Mix all the ingredients in a bowl, mashing the Stilton with the back of a fork for a smooth-ish consistency.

For the buffalo sauce, put the Frank's sauce, butter and honey in a pan. Bring to the boil, then turn the heat down and simmer for 10 minutes, stirring regularly. It needs to be thick enough to coat the wings.

Take a massive mixing bowl, shove all the wings in it, pour the sauce over and toss until every single one is coated. Serve with the blue cheese dip and celery and don't forget to wear a bib.

Tip Chicken wings have 3 sections: for this recipe they need to be divided into the tip and wingette, and the top part or drumette. Great if you can buy them like this: if not, you'll need to use a cleaver to chop off the drumette, using a chop-and-twist motion.

Chick in a Brick

Jessie **Many years ago, we resurrected our terracotta chicken brick (a long-forgotten wedding present) from the depths of the kitchen cupboard. It seems that the chicken brick has had its lay-day (if you'll excuse the pun), which is a shame, because it produces the most delicious roast chicken with a certain edge and succulence above and beyond your ordinary roast chicken. The accompanying vegetables also prove a delight as they roast and become lightly flavoured by the sweet flesh of the prunes.**

If you don't have a chicken brick, simply place everything in your roasting tin.

1 large chicken, 1.6–1.8kg

4 large carrots,
cut into chunks

3 white or red onions,
quartered

3 celery sticks,
cut into chunks

8 prunes, halved

4 garlic cloves, halved

1 lemon

1 tsp dried tarragon or
3–4 fresh tarragon sprigs
(optional)

salt and pepper

Serves 6

Soak the chicken brick, fully submerged in cold water, for at least 30 minutes. (Check the manufacturer's instructions, as some types don't need soaking.) Preheat the oven to 200°C/180°C fan/gas 6.

Once the brick has been soaked, add the chicken to one half of the brick. Scatter the carrots, onions, celery, prunes and garlic around the chicken – it may well be a snug fit, depending on the size of your brick. Squeeze the juice of the lemon over the chicken and stuff the squeezed lemon inside the chicken, along with the tarragon, if using. Season generously with salt and pepper, and cover with the other half of the brick.

Roast for around 1½–2 hours, until the meat is falling off the bones. You do not necessarily need to baste it, but you can if you like. If you want to have a more crispy skin, remove the top of the brick about 15 minutes before the end of the cooking time.

To check that the chicken is cooked, pierce the thickest part of one of the thighs with a skewer: the juices should run clear with no hint of pink. Remove the chicken and set aside to rest before carving. Using a slotted spoon, remove the vegetables and prunes to serve alongside the chicken. Add any cooking juices to your gravy, if you are serving one, or simply spoon over the chicken.

Thai Fish Cakes

Jessie   We served these to the Mayor of London when he broke Ramadan with us on the podcast back in 2018. I don't think the neighbours will ever forget the knock at their door when Sadiq Khan arrived at the wrong house with a bunch of flowers.

Lennie   I have served these at lots of our parties: they're very impressive and everyone loves them.

500g white fish, such as cod or haddock

2 tbsp fish sauce

1 tbsp Thai red curry paste

1 large egg

½ tsp caster sugar

1 tsp finely grated lime zest

1 tbsp chopped fresh coriander leaves

2 spring onions, thinly sliced

1 lemongrass stalk, tough outer leaves removed, roughly chopped

salt

flour, for dusting

vegetable oil, for frying

sweet chilli dipping sauce and lime wedges, to serve

Makes about 15

Add the fish, fish sauce, curry paste, egg, sugar, lime zest, coriander, spring onions and lemongrass to a food processor and blitz to combine. Season with the tiniest pinch of salt and blitz again. Shape the mixture into small, disc-shaped fishcakes, about 40g each, then dust in flour.

Heat the oil in a frying pan over a medium heat. When hot, fry the fishcakes in batches for about 6 minutes, turning frequently, until golden brown. Place on a piece of kitchen paper to absorb excess oil while you cook the remaining fishcakes.

Serve with sweet chilli dipping sauce and lime wedges to squeeze over the fishcakes.

Pan-Fried Sea Bass and Salsa Verde on Samphire

Lennie   I first tasted salsa verde at The River Café in Hammersmith, west London. The River Café opened in 1987 and gradually introduced everyone to delicious Italian food that went beyond just pizza and pasta. Have a fresh peach bellini too and you will almost feel you're in Italy.

Jessie   I would also serve this with Salt and Vinegar Roast Potatoes (page 54) and a salad.

4 sea bass fillets, skin on

75g unsalted butter, plus extra for the samphire

1 tbsp olive oil

200g samphire

lemon wedges to serve

salt and pepper

SALSA VERDE
120ml olive oil

3 anchovy fillets, drained

50g fresh basil, leaves picked

100g fresh parsley, leaves picked

30g fresh mint, leaves picked

2 tbsp capers

1–2 garlic cloves

2–3 Mrs Elswood sweet cucumber slices (or 6 cornichons) plus ½ tsp of the pickle juice

juice of 1 lemon

Serves 4

To make the salsa verde, put all the ingredients into a food processor (or use a hand blender) and whizz until smooth. Set aside.

Season the fish, especially the skin side. Heat a large frying pan over a medium heat. Add the butter and olive oil. Once the butter has melted and begun to sizzle, add the sea bass, skin-side down. Cook for 3–4 minutes, spooning the butter over the fish, then turn over and cook for a further minute.

Meanwhile, bring a pan of water to the boil and put the samphire in to cook for 1–2 minutes. Drain well, then toss in a little butter and season with salt and pepper.

Divide the samphire between warmed plates, put the fish on top and serve with the salsa verde, lemon wedges and some crusty bread.

Bella's Cod in Sherry with Roasted Tomatoes and Butter Beans

Jessie My husband's cousin Matt and his partner Bella live on a houseboat with their beautiful sons River and Wren. They are both excellent cooks and deftly creative. While Matt creates wistfully wild gardens, Bella conjures up brilliant clothes designs, hand puppets, the odd baby kimono and many impromptu feasts with ease and ebullience. Their boat docks near to the Towpath Cafe, a canal hole-in-the-wall that offers some of the best and most effortless food in London. I'm pretty sure the Towpath has been a positive assailant that feeds Bella's inspired but homely meal ideas, and after being a few series into *Table Manners* the podcast (and out of ideas), Bella came to the rescue with this delicious suggestion.

Don't scrimp on the ingredients: top quality produce will really make a difference to this dish. For example, I love the Brindisa Navarrico jarred butter beans – canned ones don't taste creamy enough.

250g cherry tomatoes on the vine

2–3 tbsp olive oil

4 cod fillets, skin on

1 tsp paprika

50g unsalted butter

4 shallots or 1 large red onion, finely sliced

2 Little Gem lettuce, cut into quarters lengthways

150ml manzanilla sherry

1 tbsp red wine vinegar

½ jar (about 220g) butter beans, drained

salt and pepper

Serves 4

Preheat the oven to 190°C/170°C fan/gas 5.

Keep the tomatoes on the vine and put them into a baking dish. Season and drizzle with 1 tablespoon of the olive oil, and roast in the oven for 20 minutes.

Pat the cod fillets dry with kitchen paper and season generously with salt, pepper and half of the paprika. Melt half of the butter in a large frying pan over a medium heat and cook the fish, skin-side down, for 5 minutes. Remove the fish to a plate or dish – do not clean the pan.

Add the remaining butter to the frying pan, pop in the shallots and cook over a low–medium heat for 3–4 minutes until they start to soften.

While the shallots are cooking, heat a griddle pan over a medium–high heat and add 1–2 tablespoons of olive oil. Place the lettuce pieces on the griddle pan and leave them to char until you can see dark lines forming, then turn and cook on the other side. You will need to do this in batches. Once the leaves are charred and lightly cooked but still with a bit of crunch, put them onto a plate or dish.

After the shallots have cooked for 3–4 minutes, add the sherry to the pan and turn up the heat a little to cook off the alcohol for about 2 minutes. Reduce the heat and add the remaining paprika and the vinegar.

Take the tomatoes out of the oven and add to the frying pan, keeping them on the vines as much as possible (some will have fallen off, but that's fine). Add the beans and about 120ml just-boiled water to the pan.

Return the cod to the pan, flesh-side down, along with any of its resting juices. Baste the cod with the sherry sauce and leave to cook for a few minutes. The sauce should thicken slightly but there will still be quite a bit of liquid. Finally, place the charred lettuce into the pan and leave for 2 minutes.

Serve in pasta bowls or deep plates, with some good sourdough bread to dip into the delicious sherry sauce.

See picture on the following page.

Jerk Fish Tacos with Fiery Mango Salsa

Jessie   This dish has taken some refining. Rapper and singer Stefflon Don commented on the calibre of my tacos when I served them to her, but I forgot to write down the recipe. And to be honest, I still can't remember it. The second time, my daughter didn't need to tell me if she liked it as she reached for her sippy cup and downed water. So here is my new (and improved) creation.

Mum thinks tacos should be hard and crunchy. Personally, I love the soft corn tacos you find everywhere in California, but they are harder to come across here. Tortillas can work too.

Recipe on following page.

Jerk Fish Tacos with Fiery Mango Salsa

3 cod loins,
200–250g each

5cm fresh root ginger,
grated

1 tbsp jerk spice, or
the wetter hotter jerk
seasoning (we use
Dunn's River)

3 tbsp sunflower oil

juice of 1½–2 limes

1 large red onion, sliced

2 tbsp moscatel wine
vinegar or red wine vinegar

8 medium corn or
flour tortillas

rice, avocado and finely
shredded red cabbage,
to serve

salt and pepper

MANGO SALSA
1 mango, chopped

½ red onion,
finely chopped

1 red pepper, seeded and
finely chopped

handful of chopped fresh
coriander leaves

grated zest of 1 lime,
plus juice of 3 limes

½ tsp cayenne pepper

LIME YOGHURT
100g natural yoghurt

grated zest and juice
of 1 lime

Serves 4–6 (makes 8 tacos)

Preheat the oven to 200°C/180°C fan/gas 6.

In a bowl, mix the cod with the ginger, jerk seasoning, 2 tablespoons of the sunflower oil, the juice of 1 lime and a pinch of salt. Cover and leave in the fridge for 30 minutes, if you have time.

Meanwhile, heat the remaining oil in a pan over a low heat and fry the sliced onion for a couple of minutes. Add the vinegar and cook for a few more minutes, then turn off the heat. Set aside.

To make the mango salsa, put the mango, red onion and red pepper into a mixing bowl. Add the coriander, lime zest and juice and cayenne pepper and stir until evenly mixed. Season with salt and pepper to taste.

For the lime yoghurt, mix the ingredients together and season to taste.

Place the fish and its marinade in a baking dish or roasting tin and bake for 12–15 minutes until cooked through. Break the cod into rough chunks into a serving bowl and mix in the remaining lime juice and salt and pepper to taste.

While the fish is cooking, put the tacos into the oven to warm, then wrap them loosely in foil to keep them warm.

Serve the fish immediately in a warmed taco with some lime yoghurt, red onion, sliced avocado and shredded red cabbage. Top with the mango salsa and serve rice on the side.

Jewish-ish

Lennie As a child,
Friday nights always
meant a family
meal, often with my
grandparents.

I never went out with friends
on a Friday as this was
definitely a family night.

Every week, the meal was the same: chopped liver, chicken soup
and roast chicken (nearly every part of the chicken was cooked and
eaten), followed by lokshen pudding or apple pie. The menu rarely
changed and provided for leftovers the next day so that no one had
to cook over Shabbat (Saturday). In fact, the menu for each day
of the week was the same throughout the year and there was great
excitement if my mum branched out. Latterly, my mother did cook
a more varied range of food and was an amazing cook, but I would
be disappointed if we did not have a traditional Friday-night dinner
when I visited with my own children or friends.

I still love Friday nights, although we don't all
meet up as a family as everyone does their own
thing. However, I love cooking big Friday-night
dinners for my children and their friends.
Indeed, it was probably the origin of the idea
for *Table Manners* – people coming together to
eat and chat (often ending in music and dancing
if we've all had enough to drink!).

Jessie ## For me, Jewish food is such wonderful comfort food.

It's nostalgic and tribal and a formative part of my early romance with food. Being Ashkenazi, with my grandfather coming from Russia, you get to learn about chopped liver and gefilte fish from a young age, and the scent of smoked salmon reminds me of a synagogue kiddush or a cherished Sunday in Manchester with my Grandma and bagels. Although our Friday-night dinners were never orthodox (we do not practise kosher), they were a perfect excuse to entertain and welcome a world of old and new friends into our home, sharing some of our favourite meals and enjoying the best evenings all together.

While we were shooting this book, I was made acutely aware of how passionate Mum is about food and the history of these handed-down recipes. In fact, there was a moment that we now refer to as 'Gefiltefishgate', due to her berating me – and the food stylist – for leaving the chrain dip in a jar and also not having an ironed white tablecloth. I argued that we always eat shop-bought chrain, so it seemed more accurate to show it in the jar. Mum hit back with 'Gaga would be turning in her grave right now if she knew you had served her balls with a jar!'. Needless to say, the photo you see of the fish balls on page 126 is a reshoot to accurately satisfy and honour my spirited mother and her Jewish heritage.

This chapter offers up some of our favourite Jewish foods, the ones that we believe should be tried by as many people as possible. Don't knock chopped liver until you have tried it, and don't think that salt beef or pickle-making is an impossible task. Try out Matzo Brei as a quick breakfast alternative to eggy bread and – trust us – Gaga's Chopped and Fried Gefilte Fish may change your life, but *don't* forget the serving dish for the chrain!

Matzo Brei

Lennie   Matzo is a large square cracker of unleavened flatbread that actually doesn't taste of much – it's simply flour and water – but add a slab of butter and a sharp Cheddar and it's heavenly. It is eaten all year round but is integral to the Passover story: the Jews had to leave Egypt quickly (escaping slavery and tyranny), heading for Israel, and didn't have time to wait for their bread to rise, so they settled for unleavened flatbread, which they ate in the wilderness.

My father loved Passover and used to make matzo brei for me (the only thing he would cook!). *Brei* means 'fry', so this dish is simply fried matzo. It's like eggy bread (French toast). My South African Jewish friends introduced me to a sweet version with cinnamon and sugar on the top, but I was brought up on the savoury, eating it at breakfast during Passover week when I wasn't allowed toast in the morning. It's a comforting dish, easy to make and incredibly satisfying. Don't hold back on the butter.

8 eggs

pinch of salt

8 matzo sheet crackers

butter, for frying

Serves 4–6

In a wide shallow dish, beat the eggs together with a pinch of salt.

Break up each matzo sheet into 4 pieces. Put all the matzo in a large bowl with enough cold water to cover them completely, soak for about 20–30 seconds until softened, then drain off the water.

Heat a large knob of butter in a large frying pan until hot. Dip 2 pieces of softened matzo into the beaten eggs until fully coated, then fry until the egg is cooked through. Repeat until all the matzo is cooked, adding more butter whenever the pan looks dry.

Serve immediately, either on its own or with smoked salmon, or sprinkled with sugar and a little cinnamon.

Gaga's Chopped and Fried Gefilte Fish

Jessie The smell of these will always remind me of my darling Grandma. She didn't smell of fish, she smelt sublime (Oil of Olay and Chanel Chance), but this recipe takes me back to entering her flat in Broughton Park, Manchester, when I was little. She would always make a batch for the weekend if we were going up to see her. My Grandma converted to Judaism after falling in love with my Russian-born Irish-Jewish Grandpa, but she was as Jewish as they came. She fed and fed and used more Yiddish words than anyone I know. And she was a great cook. Warning: Mum has been known to wear her shower cap and little else when making these, and to have all the doors and windows open, because the house will smell of fried fish for a day.

Lennie Gefilte fish is served at every Jewish function and celebration. You will usually find them a little sweeter than these, or you may have – unfortunately – encountered the pale, wet, miserable-looking boiled kind. This is how Gaga made them and they still beat all the rest.

500g white fish (cod was Gaga's favourite, but you can use hake, haddock or a mixture of fish)

1 small white onion, chopped

1 egg, beaten

3 tbsp medium matzo meal

small pinch of sugar (optional)

500ml sunflower oil

salt and pepper

Makes about 16 small or 8 medium balls

Mince or finely chop the fish, or put through the food processor using the round-hole grating attachment. Put it into a large bowl, add the onion and egg and mix well. Add the matzo meal, some pepper and ½ teaspoon of fine salt, and a small pinch of sugar, if you like. Mix everything together by hand until completely combined, then cover and chill for 1 hour.

With wet hands, divide the mixture into evenly sized balls. Golf-ball size for small (about 50g each or 2 heaped tablespoons of the mixture), or double that for medium-sized (don't go as big as a tennis ball). Flatten them slightly if you are making the bigger size.

Pour the oil into a medium–large pan: it should come no more than halfway up the side of the pan. Heat the oil to about 180° C – if you don't have a food thermometer, a cube of white bread dropped into the oil should turn golden in about 40 seconds.

When the oil is hot, put 4 or 5 fish balls into the pan and cook until brown (about 6 minutes for small; slightly longer for medium). You may need to turn them halfway through the cooking time. Carefully remove with a slotted spoon and drain well on kitchen paper. Repeat until all the balls are cooked.

Eat hot or cold. We like these with chrain (beetroot and horseradish sauce) or a wedge of lemon.

Lennie's Friday Night Chopped Liver

Jessie Chopped liver is a staple in Jewish households, and it also features as my starter (along with Mum's chicken soup) on my 'last supper' menu. Yes, it looks like wet cement and sounds like a *Handmaid's Tale* punishment, but I promise, it's heaven on a plate. I saw the fear in Loyle Carner's eyes when we offered this up to him, but I believe in this dish more than maybe *any* of my lyrics! It's reassuring, nostalgic, and delicious.

Lennie Have a go and trust us. You can add garlic when frying the chicken livers, but I prefer it without. Definitely try it with a sweet gherkin and a matzo cracker for the full Friday Night impact.

3 medium eggs

40g unsalted butter (or chicken fat/schmaltz, available at Jewish delis)

1 large onion, roughly chopped

250g chicken livers

salt and pepper

Serves 4–6

Put the eggs in a pan of cold water, bring to the boil and cook for 1 minute, then turn off the heat and leave them to sit in the water for about 14 minutes.

Meanwhile, heat the butter or chicken fat in a large frying pan over a medium heat and sauté the onion until just beginning to soften, about 5 minutes.

Pat the livers dry on kitchen paper and cut out any sinewy bits. Add the livers to the pan with the onion, season with salt and pepper and cook, stirring, until browned all over, about 10 minutes. Leave to cool.

Peel and roughly chop 2 of the hard-boiled eggs. Whizz the livers and onion in a food processor until quite smooth. Add the chopped eggs and whizz again until smooth.

Put the chopped liver on a plate and smooth out to an even layer, reaching the edge of the plate. Grate the remaining egg over the top.

Serve with fresh challah bread or matzo and pickled cucumbers.

Latkes

Jessie Latkes are basically Jewish hash browns. Traditionally served around Hanukkah (our Festival of Lights), these shallow-fried potato pancakes can be dressed up or served simply as a perfect comfort food. At Russ & Daughters, probably my favourite New York Jewish deli, they serve them with sour cream and apple sauce. That's the usual way. However, we've also had them with smoked salmon and caviar. They are definitely not slimming, but the deliciousness is absolutely worth it. To get them really tasty, do them last minute and get ready to stink the house out, as well as drowning out any chance of kitchen conversation.

6 medium–large potatoes, about 1.5kg (Maris Piper work well), peeled

1 white onion, grated

2 medium eggs, beaten

about 150ml rapeseed or sunflower oil, for frying

salt and pepper

Makes 16

Coarsely grate the potatoes, using a box grater or the grating attachment on a food processor, then place in a sieve or a clean tea towel/piece of muslin and squeeze or wring out as much moisture as possible.

Tip the potato into a large mixing bowl and add the grated onion and eggs. Using your hands, mix everything together and season with plenty of pepper and at least 1 teaspoon of salt.

Heat 3–4 tablespoons of oil in a large heavy-based frying pan over a medium–high heat. Take heaped tablespoonfuls of the mixture (about 60g each) and add to the hot oil, cooking 4 latkes at a time. Turn the heat down to medium, gently press the latkes down with a spatula and fry for 4–5 minutes on each side until golden. Drain on kitchen paper while you cook the rest of the latkes, adding more oil for each batch. You can keep the latkes warm in a low oven while you finish cooking.

Serve immediately.

Chicken Soup

Lennie Every Jewish family thinks their mother's chicken soup is the best. In emergencies, I have been known to send my soup across London in a taxi, because this 'Jewish penicillin' most definitely has healing qualities.

Reminiscent of Friday nights spent with family when I was a girl, the fragrance of the simmering soup is delicious. Chicken soup is synonymous with every Jewish household, and is one of the things that makes me most proud to be Jewish.

Serve with matzo crackers and challah bread.

2kg chicken thighs and legs

5 large onions, skins left on, halved, cutting off the rooty bit

8 carrots, sliced about 2–3cm thick

4 celery sticks, with leaves, halved

1 leek, halved

½ swede

2 tbsp Telma Chicken Soup Mix (available from a kosher shop or online), or 2 good-quality chicken stock cubes

1 tsp whole black peppercorns

1 tsp salt

Matzo Balls (see opposite), to serve

Serves 6 (makes about 2 litres)

Put the chicken and all the vegetables in a stockpot or very large pan (about 4 litres capacity) with enough cold water to cover everything by about 5cm (about 3 litres) and bring to the boil. When boiling, skim off all the frothy scum until there is none left. Add the soup mix or stock cubes, the peppercorns and salt, bring back to the boil and then reduce the heat and gently simmer for 2–3 hours.

Season the soup to taste, then leave to cool. Pour the soup through a colander into a large bowl. Carefully retrieve the carrots from the colander and add back to the soup. Give everything else a good squeeze to release the juices. Some people put a little of the chicken into the soup, but I'm not sure it has much taste after being boiled for so long – and you will make your cat/dog very happy if you give them the bone-free chicken meat.

Put the clear soup and carrots into the fridge for at least 2 hours or overnight. When it's well chilled the fat will rise to the top and you can easily skim it off.

To serve, bring the soup to the boil over a medium heat and add your cooked matzo balls just before serving.

Tip The soup may not be completely clear (and it doesn't really matter), but if you want to make it as clear as a consommé then you can either put it all through a tea strainer (as I did when Jay Rayner was our guest) or you can use one or two egg shells from the matzo balls and put them in the soup as you bring it back to the boil – fish out the egg shells before you put the matzo balls in.

Matzo Balls

Lennie

In the words of Marilyn Monroe: 'Isn't there any other part of the matzo you can eat?'

It has taken me ages to achieve light fluffy matzo balls, but I think after 40-odd years of making them I have finally managed it. Of course, you can cheat and use the ready-made packets, which are sometimes sold under the name 'kneidl'.

Matzo balls are very divisive: some prefer them fluffy like clouds, some prefer them dense like bullets. Some have them in the soup, others save them till after. But if you start by saying 'I'll only have one' you will always submit to the second. Delicious and *crucial* to Chicken Soup.

100g medium matzo meal

1 tsp baking powder

pinch of salt

pinch of white pepper

3 large eggs, beaten

1 tbsp rapeseed oil

4 tbsp hot Chicken Soup (see opposite) or boiling water

Makes about 15 balls

Put all the dry ingredients in a bowl, gradually stir in the eggs and oil and then gradually add the chicken soup, mixing until smooth. Cover the bowl and chill for 30 minutes – it will firm up slightly.

Line a tray with baking parchment. Bring a large pan of salted water to the boil.

Wet your fingers and take small pieces of the mixture to make soft balls, about 2cm in diameter, placing them on the lined tray until you have used up all the mixture.

Drop the balls into the boiling water, turn down the heat and gently simmer for about 20–25 minutes until they are soft. They should swell up slightly, rise to the surface and look like little clouds.

Lift out using a slotted spoon and serve them in chicken soup.

See picture on the following page.

Easy-Peasy Chicken or Turkey Schnitzel

Jessie

This is easy to make, yet so flavourful and comforting. It can be eaten in a sandwich, or with mashed potato and apple sauce, or you can go Italian and serve it with spaghetti and tomato sauce as Chicken Milanese. Plonk a fried egg on top and it becomes a Holstein. Versatile and tasty, it is basically a posh chicken nugget, so it even appeases my toddler's beige food habit.

4 small boneless skinless chicken breasts (about 150g each) or 4 turkey breast escalopes

100g plain flour

2 eggs

100g dried panko breadcrumbs

4 tbsp grated Parmesan

75ml rapeseed or sunflower oil, for frying

salt and pepper

Serves 4

Place each chicken (or turkey) breast between 2 sheets of clingfilm and beat with a rolling pin until flattened – about 5mm thick all over.

You will need 3 large shallow bowls. Put the flour in one bowl and season with salt and pepper. Break the eggs into the second bowl and beat lightly. In the third bowl, mix the breadcrumbs and Parmesan.

Dip each chicken breast in the flour to coat it all over, then dip into the egg to coat on both sides. Finally, coat it with the breadcrumbs and Parmesan. Put on a plate or a tray lined with baking parchment and chill until ready to use.

Heat the oil in a large frying pan over a medium–high heat and fry the schnitzels for about 3 minutes on each side until golden brown: you will probably need to do this in batches. Drain on kitchen paper and keep warm while you cook the remaining schnitzels.

Serve with a fresh salad, coleslaw and sweet potato fries, or with Parmesan and Spring Onion Mash (page 55) and a fried egg.

Chicken with Apricots

Lennie

My friend Gill is a brilliant cook who has all sorts of tricks up her sleeve to make things tasty and easy. She is from South Africa, where lots of interesting dishes seem to have originated. I love this dish because it's quick, simple and requires so few ingredients, but the flavour is fabulous.

12 skin-on chicken thighs

125g apricot chutney
(Mrs Ball's is good; also
see tip, below)

400g tin apricots in juice

3 tbsp onion soup powder
(we use Osem Onion Soup
Mix; also see tip, below)

salt and pepper

Serves 6

Preheat the oven to 200°C/180°C fan/gas 6.

Put the chicken in a baking dish. Combine the chutney, apricots and their juice and the onion soup powder and pour the mixture over the chicken. Season with salt and pepper.

Bake for about 1 hour until the chicken is cooked and the sauce is brown and sticky. If it is browning too quickly, turn down the oven and cover the dish with foil. Serve hot, with rice.

Tip   If using another chutney, such as mango, add 2 tablespoons of apricot jam. If you can't find onion soup powder, you could substitute a good shake of onion granules or a very finely chopped onion.

Salt Beef

Lennie For this, you need salted brisket, which isn't the easiest to find, but good butchers will do it if you order it in advance. You won't get it from supermarket butchers. I have bought it from kosher butchers. It's quite a hassle to salt it yourself – the brining process takes several days.

piece of salted (brined) brisket, about 1.5kg

1 tbsp whole black peppercorns

5–6 bay leaves

Serves 6–8

Put the brisket into a large stockpot or saucepan, add enough cold water to cover and bring to the boil.

Tip out the hot water and then add enough fresh cold water to cover the beef, this time adding the peppercorns and bay leaves. Bring to the boil, then reduce the heat to a simmer and cook for about 2½ hours.

Drain off the water and your salt beef is ready. Carve into thick slices and serve with pickled cucumbers, a good strong mustard (I like English mustard with this) and Kugel (page 143) or Latkes (page 130). Sauerkraut from a jar or a nice fresh Coleslaw (page 143) goes well too.

Currant and Apple Coleslaw

Jessie

A sweet yet tangy coleslaw to serve with Salt Beef (page 140), shove in a sandwich with a sharp Cheddar, or dollop onto a baked potato.

½ small cabbage

3 carrots

2 spring onions

1 Granny Smith apple

3 tbsp mayonnaise

3 tbsp Greek yoghurt

2 tsp Dijon mustard

juice of ½ lemon

2 tbsp currants or raisins

salt and pepper

Serves 4

Grate or finely slice the cabbage, carrots, spring onions and apple – or grate them all together in a food processor.

Tip the grated vegetables into a bowl, add all the remaining ingredients and stir thoroughly. Season to taste. Chill until ready to serve.

Kugel

Lennie

Kugel is potato pudding. We would have it on Friday night instead of roast potatoes with chicken, brisket or salt beef. It's delicious, with a crispy outside and a moist pudding-like portion of soft potatoes and onions in the middle. Bake it slowly so it doesn't burn on top.

6 medium–large potatoes, about 1.5kg (Maris Piper work well), peeled and coarsely grated

1 white onion, coarsely grated

4 medium eggs, beaten

5 tbsp rapeseed or sunflower oil

salt and pepper

Serves 6–8

Preheat the oven to 200°C/180°C fan/gas 6.

Place the grated potatoes in a sieve or a clean tea towel/piece of muslin and squeeze or wring out as much moisture as possible. Tip the potato into a large mixing bowl and add the grated onion and eggs. Using your hands, mix everything together and season with plenty of pepper and at least 1 teaspoon of salt.

Pour 4 tablespoons of the oil into a 1.5-litre baking dish, then tip in the potato mixture. Sprinkle the remaining oil over the top. Cover with foil and bake for 20 minutes, then remove the foil and bake for another 40 minutes until the kugel is crispy brown on top. Serve hot.

Brisket in Cola

Lennie

Brisket is often served in America at Jewish holidays, and the American sister trio band, Haim, reminisced about their mother's brisket with red wine on the podcast. I've always found that cola worked wonderfully with brisket and surprisingly doesn't taste too sweet.

Buy the brisket flat (rather than rolled) and trim off the excess fat, or ask the butcher to do so, and use regular cola, not diet, for the best flavour. Serve with mashed potatoes or Kugel (page 143). This is just as good the next day, if not better.

2kg brisket

1 tbsp rapeseed or sunflower oil

3–4 onions, sliced

3 garlic cloves, crushed

500ml cola

400g tomato ketchup

4 tsp onion granules

2 tsp light brown sugar

fine salt and pepper

Serves 8–10

Preheat the oven to 150°C/130°C fan/gas 2.

Rub the brisket all over with fine salt. Heat the oil in a large heavy-based frying pan, then fry the brisket for 4 minutes on each side until browned.

Put the onions in a roasting tin and put the brisket on top, fat-side up. Mix together all the other ingredients and pour over the meat. Cover the tin with a sheet of baking parchment or greaseproof paper and then cover with foil, sealing it tightly around the edges of the tin. Cook for about 3½–4 hours until the meat is tender.

Remove from the oven and leave to stand, still covered with foil, for about 30 minutes.

Slice the meat against the grain and serve with the sauce poured over.

Quick Cucumber and Fennel Pickles

Jessie   I always have a jar of Mrs Elswood Haimisha Cucumbers in my fridge, much to my husband's dismay. But one day I ran out of them and decided to improvise. From an old bit of fennel and a sad cucumber I created a pickle that is perfect in a Cheddar cheese sandwich, or with salt beef or cold meats. This is quick to make and can be eaten after a few hours, but can also be stored in the fridge for weeks.

150ml warm water

50g sugar (preferably brown)

200ml red wine vinegar

2 tsp yellow mustard seeds

1 tsp ground turmeric

1½ large cucumbers (about 600g), halved lengthways and finely sliced

½ fennel bulb, finely sliced

3 shallots, finely sliced

handful of chopped dill

1 tbsp salt

Makes 1 very large (at least 1-litre) Kilner jar

Put the water and sugar into a measuring jug or bowl. Let stand for 10 minutes, stirring occasionally, until the sugar has dissolved. Add the vinegar, mustard seeds and turmeric, mix thoroughly and set aside.

Place the cucumbers, fennel and shallots in a bowl and add the dill and the salt. Pour over the pickling liquid and mix the ingredients well, then transfer to a large preserving jar, seal and put in the fridge. Leave for at least 3–4 hours, turning occasionally if the pickling mixture doesn't quite cover the vegetables at first.

Summer time

Jessie ## Summer is my favourite time to cook.

As soon as the clocks go forward, I am ready to re-open my door to feed friends, or wander along our local East-End high road, Kingsland Road, which is lined with Turkish grills, happy-hour taco spots and late-night drinking haunts with watermelon margaritas. It's full of brilliant places to buy food and eat out, tempting you out of the house with the waft of meat on an open grill.

Mum loves to get the gas barbecue out as soon as we have one day over 10°C and rain does not deter the promise of a Sunday 'summer' meat mêlée. You will find her with an umbrella and cagoule, barking orders through the window while we watch on inside, warm and dry. The spread is enormous and my poor brother Alex will be taking cold charred lamb chops for his packed lunch for days and days after.

We spend almost every summer holiday on the Greek island of Skopelos. I anticipate that first taste of a Greek peach with thick yoghurt and Skopelos honey, the fried courgettes and *skordalia* (garlic sauce) in Molos, meatballs in ouzo at International Café, feta in filo with drizzled honey at Agnanti, the life-changing orange flan at our beloved Rodi, and the last-chance saloon gyros you run to get at Platanos Square before getting on the boat and bidding farewell to the island that has shaped our summers.

Skopelos has given my family many an unforgettable dinner moment. I remember the mojito with wild mint I sipped at sundown, moments before my husband asked me to marry him. I remember it so well because, while drinking, I silently thought how it would make the perfect aperitif for a Skopelos wedding, *hopefully* my wedding. My husband and I still laugh at the self-induced stomach ulcer he gave himself after consuming too many honey balls and Mythos beers one summer, making our freshly engaged love nest slightly less amorous.

Although many of the recipes in this chapter bring us back to late-summer Skopelos holidays, summer really is the best time to have people round and to have fun cooking. There's always plenty of dishes laid out at a summer do, which makes the glutton in me jump for joy; you can avoid an awkward table plan, with everyone sprawled out into the garden; and you don't have to worry about serving the food hot, which is helpful as my husband still hasn't mastered our kettle barbecue. So many dishes can be made in advance and you will have leftover salads and cold meats for the next day.

Lennie This chapter has meals that have been passed down through the years and different countries, inspiring many a beautiful summer spread.

I am definitely a summer person. I love light evenings with the French windows open onto the garden and the possibility of eating outside. It always tastes better.

Summer cooking is light eating, barbecues, picnics, salads and fun. Summer desserts are really the only ones I like. I will always make room for a tangy summer pudding, Eton mess or any flavour of ice cream.

Greece is so wonderful for fruits and vegetables: a fragrant fuzzy peach can be eaten on its own and a Greek tomato will never let you down. Skopelos never fails to fill my soul with joy and revive my spirits when I arrive, tired, and see the beautiful town rising up from the sea. On our island there is absolute pride in the sourcing and cooking of local ingredients – a forager's dream. True, the menus don't change much, but there is a comfort in knowing that, on your first night there, you will drink local pink wine, eat tzatziki and have a Greek salad with delicious grilled local fish.

I hope you enjoy these summer recipes, which can be enjoyed no matter what country you are in. There are zesty side dishes, handed-down and adored Greek recipes, burgers for the barbecue and vibrant salads.

Bouyiourdi Eggs

Bouyiourdi is a Greek favourite and can be served as a side without eggs. Our favourite beach taverna at Limnonari on Skopelos serves it with baked eggs – it's a Greek version of the Middle-Eastern dish shakshuka.

3–4 tbsp olive oil

1 large onion, thinly sliced

2 red peppers, seeded and roughly chopped

1 red chilli, thinly sliced

400g tin chopped tomatoes

2 tsp caster sugar

1 tsp ground cinnamon

1 tsp ground cumin

1 tsp sweet paprika

1 tbsp chopped fresh thyme

1 tbsp dried oregano or chopped fresh oregano leaves, plus a little extra as wished

small handful of chopped fresh mint, plus extra to serve

6 tomatoes, thinly sliced

200g feta, crumbled

6 eggs

salt and pepper

Serves 6

Preheat the oven to 180°C/160°C fan/gas 4.

Heat 1–2 tablespoons of the olive oil in a large frying pan over a medium heat and fry the onion, peppers and chilli for about 4–5 minutes until they begin to soften. Place in a large baking dish (about 2 litres capacity) and season with salt and pepper.

Pour in the chopped tomatoes, add the sugar, spices, herbs and some salt and pepper and stir to mix. Place the sliced tomatoes on top of the mixture and drizzle over a generous glug of olive oil. Bake for 25 minutes.

Crumble the feta over the tomatoes and sprinkle over a little more oregano. Cook for a further 10 minutes.

Take the dish out of the oven and turn the oven up to 200°C/180°C fan/gas 6. Using a tablespoon, make six little hollows in the sauce and crack in the eggs. Bake for a further 10–15 minutes, depending on how you like your eggs.

Scatter over some fresh mint and serve immediately, with a dollop of Greek yoghurt or Labneh (page 186) and some good fresh bread or flatbread to soak up the sauce.

Lennie's Puy Lentil Salad

Jessie   **Mum has been making this dish since the 1990s, and it's one of those recipes that everyone asks for once they've tasted it. It's perfect for a summer do, barbecue or a 'bring a dish' party.**

Lennie   **Blitzing the veg in a food processor makes this super-easy to prepare.**

4 tbsp olive oil

1 large onion,
finely chopped

1 celery stick,
finely chopped

1 carrot,
finely chopped

2 garlic cloves,
finely chopped

250g Puy lentils

500ml chicken stock

2 tbsp wholegrain mustard

2 tbsp balsamic vinegar

200g feta

salt and pepper

Serves 4–6 as a side

Heat the olive oil in a frying pan over a medium heat and sauté the onion, celery, carrot and garlic until the onion is translucent. Add the lentils and stir to coat them in the oil, then add the chicken stock. Cover with a lid and cook for about 25 minutes until the lentils are soft. Keep an eye on them towards the end of the cooking time, in case the lentils catch when most of the liquid has been absorbed.

Take the pan off the heat, stir in the mustard and balsamic vinegar and season with salt and pepper to taste.

Put the lentils into a serving dish, crumble the feta over the top and serve.

See picture on the following page.

Roasted Pickled Carrot Salad with Ricotta and Rocket

Jessie There is a beautiful music venue in Copenhagen called Vega. I appreciate the hallmark Scandinavian architecture, but I wonder whether Bowie, Prince or Björk loved playing there as much as I do because of the backstage catering. Originally called The People's House, it was the home of the Danish Workers' Union movement and that history seeps through the open kitchen where the crew, band and promoters all sit eating together, with plate upon plate of seasonal delights. The smells of lunch would already be wafting through while you ate your breakfast. There was something so warm and homely about the set-up that I wouldn't feel as homesick as I often do on tour.

This is a version of one of the many delicious things I have had at Vega. On the podcast, we served this along with other salads and a plate of Rare Roast Beef Salad (page 163).

150ml red wine vinegar

4 tbsp sugar

1 tbsp salt

1 tsp juniper berries

4 star anise

500g small–medium carrots, peeled

1½ tbsp rapeseed oil

60–100g rocket

100g ricotta

handful of pumpkin or sunflower seeds

extra virgin olive oil and apple cider vinegar, to serve

salt and pepper

Serves 4–6 as a side

Put the vinegar, sugar, salt, juniper berries and star anise in a large pan and add 500ml cold water to create a pickling juice. Add the carrots and bring the water to the boil, then turn off the heat and leave the carrots in the liquid for 30 minutes.

Preheat the oven to 200°C/180°C fan/gas 6.

Drain the carrots, place them in a roasting tin with the rapeseed oil and toss to coat the carrots in oil. Season with salt and pepper. Roast for 30–40 minutes until they are beginning to brown. Leave to cool down.

Make a bed of rocket leaves on a serving plate. Add the roasted carrots (they can still be slightly warm) and scatter over some crumbled ricotta and pumpkin or sunflower seeds. Drizzle with a little olive oil and cider vinegar and serve.

See picture on the following page.

Rare Roast Beef Salad

Jessie   I remember when Mum purchased a meat slicer especially for this dish. It took up half the kitchen and made her look extremely professional, but there was always the faint chance of a finger getting sliced in the process.

Lennie   Before I had a meat slicer I had been known to take the roast beef back to the meat counter at the local supermarket and ask them to slice it. That demands chutzpah. For this dish the apparatus is a bonus, but if you don't have it, slice the meat as thinly as you can with a sharp carving knife. If you do have a meat slicer, a piece of good topside is ideal for this, otherwise buy a better cut such as fillet or sirloin. The rarer the meat the softer the slice – and don't hold back on the Parmesan shavings.

We served this up for the trio who create the *My Dad Wrote a Porno* podcast, among an array of salads and sides, including the Roasted Pickled Carrot Salad (page 159). It's a winner for a light picking lunch or dinner.

750g–1kg topside, fillet or sirloin

1 tbsp olive oil

60g rocket

60g watercress

extra virgin olive oil, to drizzle

50–75g Parmesan, shaved

salt and pepper

Serves 6–8

Remove the meat from the fridge at least 30 minutes before cooking to bring it to room temperature.

Preheat the oven to 220°C/200°C fan/gas 7.

Season the beef with salt and pepper.

Heat a small heavy roasting tin or ovenproof frying pan over a high heat. Add the olive oil and sear the beef on all sides for about 3–5 minutes in total, rendering any fat.

Transfer to the oven and roast for 30–45 minutes, depending how rare you like the beef.

Leave to rest. When cool, chill in the fridge, preferably overnight.

Slice the beef as thinly as possible. Make a bed of rocket and watercress on a serving plate and top with the beef. Season to taste, adding a good glug of extra virgin olive oil, and finish with shavings of Parmesan.

Spanakopita

Jessie

A staple in every Greek bakery at any hour. During our summers on the island of Skopelos, plenty were scoffed after a night at the local discotheque and too many White Russians. Moreish and light, it will be gone in moments.

Lennie

You can also use this filling to make samosa-style parcels like the Spicy Lamb in Filo on page 170.

3 tbsp olive oil

1 onion, finely chopped

1kg frozen whole leaf spinach, defrosted

small bunch of parsley, finely chopped

small bunch of fresh dill, finely chopped

200g feta, crumbled

180g cream cheese

2 large eggs, lightly beaten

about ¼ nutmeg, freshly grated

60g unsalted butter, melted, for brushing

250–270g pack of filo pastry (7 sheets)

salt and pepper

Serves 8

Heat the olive oil in a large frying pan and sauté the onion for 8–10 minutes until soft.

Squeeze out as much water as you can from the spinach and pat dry on kitchen paper; you should end up with about 400g. Add the spinach to the pan with the onion and cook for about 3 minutes. Add the parsley, dill, and some salt and pepper. Cook over a low heat for 1–2 minutes, then leave to cool.

Preheat the oven to 200°C/180°C fan/gas 6.

Add the feta, cream cheese, eggs and nutmeg to the cooled spinach mixture.

Butter a large baking dish (a rectangular one about 22 × 33cm, or a round or oval one of about 3 litres capacity) and line with 4 sheets of filo pastry, brushing each sheet with butter. The pastry should overlap and hang over the sides of the baking dish.

Tip the spinach mixture into the dish and spread out until level. Bring the edges of the filo pastry over the spinach mixture and then cover the mixture with the remaining 3 sheets of crumpled filo. Brush the crumpled filo with the remaining butter.

Bake for about 20–25 minutes until the pie is golden. Leave to stand for 15 minutes before serving.

Griddled Asparagus with Pistachios and Cheddar

Jessie

Near where I live in London, I have a favourite local coffee shop that serves the best breakfast in Hackney. It's called Esther's and it's one of the few places I could happily sit on my own all day, talking to the baristas and sampling everything on the menu. It's a place I proudly take people to and know they will become instant fans. One rainy summer's morning I went in and had something like this with a soft-boiled egg and sourdough – a great breakfast dish. You could also add some griddled courgettes to beef it up, and the asparagus would work well on the barbecue.

2 tbsp olive oil

400g asparagus, woody ends removed

50g raw shelled pistachios

2 tbsp finely chopped mint leaves

grated zest and juice of 1 lemon

50g good strong Cheddar (Lincolnshire Poacher is great), crumbled or coarsely grated

glug of extra virgin olive oil, to serve

salt and pepper

Serves 4 as a side

Heat a griddle pan over a high heat. (Put the extractor fan on: the asparagus creates quite a lot of smoke.) If you don't have a griddle, use a frying pan, but the griddle makes those nice black char lines on the veg. Add the olive oil and, when it's hot, add the asparagus to the pan and leave for 4–5 minutes, so you get the griddle marks. Turn the asparagus over and cook for a further 1–2 minutes until tender but still with a bit of crunch.

In a pestle and mortar, bash the pistachios until crumbly, then mix in the mint and the lemon zest and a little salt and pepper.

Place the asparagus on a serving plate and scatter over the crumbled pistachio mix, then the Cheddar. Add a little more salt and pepper, a drizzle of extra virgin olive oil and squeeze over the lemon juice.

See picture on the following page.

Griddled Baby Leeks with Feta

A light vegetarian side dish that is tangy and pretty to serve up along with other dishes.

20 baby leeks

1–2 tbsp olive oil

1 tsp fresh thyme leaves

2 tbsp chopped fresh mint

grated zest of 1 lemon

80g feta, crumbled

glug of extra virgin olive oil, to serve

salt and pepper

Serves 4 as a side

Bring a large pan of salted water to the boil and put the leeks in to blanch for 2 minutes. Drain on kitchen paper.

Heat a griddle pan over a high heat. Add the olive oil and some of the blanched baby leeks – you will need to do this in batches. Cook for 3–4 minutes on each side, until tender and marked with lovely black char lines.

Once you have cooked all the leeks, place them on a serving plate and scatter with the thyme, mint and lemon zest. Crumble the feta over the top, drizzle with extra virgin olive oil, and season with salt and pepper.

See picture on the following page.

Spicy Lamb in Filo

Lennie

The Greeks love a pie. They will fill them with anything from spinach and cream cheese to meat. They even have a 'milk pie'. I first made this as a quick pie for a New Year's Day lunch with friends. It went down a treat. Don't be afraid of filo pastry, it works if you show a little confidence. It's perfect for samosa-style parcels, as here, or you could also use this filling to make a larger pie, following the method for Spanakopita (page 164).

750g minced lamb (look for a low fat content)

2 red onions, chopped

4 large garlic cloves, crushed

2 tsp ground cumin

1 tsp ground cinnamon

2 tsp medium-hot paprika

50g pine nuts

3 tbsp rose harissa paste

150g feta

2 tbsp roughly chopped flat-leaf parsley

grated zest of 1 lemon

250g pack of filo pastry

60g unsalted butter, melted, for brushing

salt and pepper

TAHINI YOGHURT
2 tbsp tahini

250g natural yoghurt

½ lemon

Makes 16–20 parcels

Preheat the oven to 200°C/180°C fan/gas 6.

Heat a large non-stick frying pan, add the lamb and fry until browned, about 6–8 minutes.

Stir in the onions and garlic and fry for 5–10 minutes until the onions have softened. Add the spices and pine nuts and cook for another 2 minutes, then stir in the harissa. Season to taste, remove from the heat and set aside to cool.

Crumble the feta into the lamb mixture, add the parsley and lemon zest and mix well.

Unfold the filo pastry and cut into long strips, about 10 × 30cm. Take the first strip and brush with melted butter (see the step-by-step pictures, overleaf). Put a spoonful of the lamb mixture near the bottom of the first strip, then fold a corner of the pastry over it to form a triangle. Continue folding the pastry upwards in triangles to enclose the filling and create a triangular parcel; pinch the edges together and place on a baking sheet. Continue until you have used all the filling, then brush all the parcels with the remaining butter.

Bake for about 15 minutes or until golden and crisp.

Whisk the tahini and yoghurt together in a bowl. Add a squeeze of lemon and season to taste. Serve the tahini yoghurt with the filo parcels.

1

2

4

172　　SUMMERTIME

3

Meatballs with Ouzo

Jessie There is a café on the waterfront in Skopelos town where we love to go. It's called the International Café and it's run by our friend Yanni. 'Meet you at brown chairs' (as it's also known) would be a common message to each other pre- or post-dinner. In our younger years, we would go there for towering ice-cream sundaes and *karidopita* (walnut cake); as teenagers, my sister and I would glug Amaretto Sours before waiting another 4 hours until the clubs got busy. Mum always orders a Brandy Alexander. Nowadays, as an ever-expanding family, we can be found sitting watching the sunset ferries come in, enjoying carafes of rosé, small town gossip, honey balls and 'one more drink', laughing until closing time. There are so many recipes from this unassuming treasure of a café that I could offer: this one is our take on Yanni's mother's divine meatballs.

3 slices white bread (about 100g), crusts removed

500g lean minced lamb

1 large egg, beaten

1 large onion, finely chopped

1 garlic clove, crushed

1 tbsp finely chopped flat-leaf parsley

2 tbsp finely chopped fresh mint

1 tbsp dried oregano

150g unsalted butter

200ml ouzo

150ml hot lamb stock

salt and pepper

Serves 4 (makes about 32 meatballs)

Preheat the oven to 180°C/160°C fan/gas 4.

Soak the bread in cold water to soften for about 10 minutes, then squeeze out the excess water. Put the lamb in a bowl, add the bread, egg, onion, garlic and herbs, salt and pepper, and mix well. Wet your hands, then form the mixture into small meatballs, about 3cm in diameter.

Place the meatballs in a baking dish or roasting tin just large enough to hold them in a single layer. Bake for 30 minutes.

Melt the butter in a large frying pan over a medium heat, then add the meatballs and their cooking juices, stirring until they are well coated in butter, and fry for about 3 minutes. Add the ouzo and stir to incorporate, then add the stock. Simmer for about 3 minutes, moving the meatballs around so they are all flavoured with ouzo.

Serve the meatballs with the juices from the pan, either with rice (better for soaking up the juices) or chips (as they often do in Greece) and a nice Greek salad.

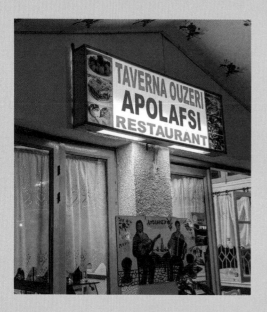

Beef Stifado

Lennie

As a Greek aficionado, I love beef stifado (if you will pardon the rhyme!). The aroma of cinnamon and nutmeg is divine and always reminds me of looking into the kitchen at the tavernas in Greece when you go to choose your evening meal. This is an easy dish to make and very delicious.

1kg good-quality stewing beef, cut into largish chunks

2 tbsp olive oil

1 large onion, chopped

3 garlic cloves, chopped

200ml red wine

1 cinnamon stick

a good grating of fresh nutmeg or ½ tsp ground nutmeg

1 beef stock cube

2–3 bay leaves

400g tin chopped tomatoes

1 tbsp tomato purée

500g (about 15) little shallots or baby onions, peeled

salt and pepper

Serves 8

Remove the meat from the fridge at least 30 minutes before cooking.

Preheat the oven to 170°C/150°C fan/gas 3.

Heat 1 tablespoon of the olive oil in a large casserole over a medium–high heat. Season the meat and sear, in batches, turning until browned on all sides. Using a slotted spoon, remove the meat from the pan and set aside.

Add the remaining olive oil to the pan and, when hot, add the onion and garlic and cook for 5 minutes until softened. Add the wine and cook for 2 minutes, then add the cinnamon, nutmeg, stock cube, bay leaves, tomatoes, tomato purée and 200ml water. Season with salt and pepper.

Return the meat to the pan, stir to mix, then cover the casserole and cook in the oven for 1 hour.

Remove the lid, add the shallots and cook, uncovered, for another 1 hour, stirring halfway through.

Serve with orzo pasta, rice or mashed potatoes. It will be even better the next day and also freezes well.

Babybel Bifteki Burgers

Jessie Living in Dalston in east London, I can step out of my house on any day of the year and be greeted by the whiff of charcoal and meat. And I love it. It reminds me of summer, barbecues and going out wet-haired and pink-cheeked for a holiday meal.

Bifteki is an aromatic meatball burger you get in Greece: it is often stuffed with feta and it can be oven-grilled among sliced potatoes. Mum started making these a few years ago. The Babybel adds an oozy chewy centre that will make you give the cheese a new level of appreciation.

1kg minced steak/beef
(about 20 per cent fat)

2 tbsp fresh oregano leaves
or dried oregano

2 tbsp tomato ketchup

3 tbsp onion granules or
1 finely chopped red onion

8 Babybel cheeses

burger buns, lettuce and
sliced tomato, to serve
(optional)

salt and pepper

Makes 8

Season the meat with salt and pepper and add the oregano, ketchup and onion. Using your hands, combine until evenly mixed.

Take a Babybel and shape the meat around it to form a burger, ensuring that the cheese is completely covered. Chill for 1 hour.

Cook the burgers on a hot barbecue until the outside is browned, the meat is cooked through and the cheese is beginning to melt and seep through. You can also pan-fry or grill them if you don't have a barbecue. Serve immediately, on their own, or with salad, rice or chips, or in buns with lettuce and tomato.

Chicken Paillard

Lennie **This is so easy, summery and full of flavour. You make it at the last minute, so get your side dishes ready first. Don't skimp on the butter – it's what makes the sauce so delicious.**

4 boneless skinless
chicken breasts

50g unsalted butter

juice of 2 lemons

bunch of basil leaves

salt and pepper

Serves 4

Put each chicken breast on a piece of clingfilm or greaseproof paper, allowing enough room for the chicken to spread as you beat it. Using a rolling pin, beat the chicken until it is flat and very thin: about 3mm.

Melt half the butter in a large frying pan over a medium–high heat. You will need to cook the chicken in batches, using the other half of the butter for the second batch. If you can't fit 2 of the flattened breasts in your frying pan that's fine, just cook one at a time – they don't take long. Fry the chicken for about 3–4 minutes, turning frequently and turning the heat down slightly after they go into the pan. Season with salt and pepper while you're cooking them. Remove the cooked chicken to a plate.

When all the breasts are done, squeeze the lemon juice into the pan with the butter and add the basil leaves. Return the chicken to the pan to coat it in the juices.

Serve with new potatoes and salads of your choice.

Salmon with Ginger and Coriander Crumb

Lennie

Jessie likes to add a red chilli to the breadcrumbs and coriander; I don't like heat so I don't do it, but it's delicious either way. Serve with a nice green salad – rocket, spinach and watercress would be good – and small new potatoes.

small side of salmon (about 800g) or 4 individual pieces, skin on

8cm fresh root ginger, peeled and grated

3 spring onions, finely chopped

85g dried panko breadcrumbs

about 25g fresh coriander, chopped

1 red chilli, seeded and finely diced (optional)

2 tbsp olive oil

salt and pepper

Serves 4

Preheat the oven to 200°C/180°C fan/gas 6.

Rinse the salmon and dry with kitchen paper. Place it skin-side down in a baking tin and season with salt and pepper.

Spread the ginger and spring onions evenly over the salmon.

Stir the breadcrumbs together with the coriander, chilli, if using, and olive oil and spread the mixture evenly over the salmon, pressing gently.

Bake for 15 minutes until the breadcrumbs are golden.

Serve immediately.

Labneh

Jessie Become a cheese-maker with very little effort and impress everyone. Labneh is a Middle-Eastern strained yoghurt cheese. It can be served savoury or sweet and it goes well with shakshuka or Bouyiourdi Eggs (page 154) or with flatbread as a dip as part of a mezze spread. It's very versatile and you can experiment with different flavours. In Los Angeles, there's a farmers' market that does the most gorgeous fig labneh, which is basically fresh figs and honey, so get creative!

Lennie We served this up to the charming Michelin-starred chef Tom Kerridge with a harissa shakshuka for brunch. Jessie thought mine was too solid and wanted to add olive oil to make it more liquid and to add some herbs. We disagreed and served Tom Kerridge both. Mine looked better and a lot more appetising (Jessie said I sabotaged hers by not showing it as much love in presentation). Tom told us to add water to loosen the cheese if necessary, which seemed a bit odd as I'd spent all night getting the water out. But he does have the Michelin stars. If it's quite solid, you can roll it into little balls and put it into a bowl with olive oil poured around it – it will keep in the fridge like this for several days. If you're going savoury, serve your labneh with herbs or spices – try cayenne, oregano, sumac, za'atar or dukkah.

You will need some cheesecloth or muslin and some string.

500g full-fat Greek yoghurt

½ tsp salt

TO SERVE
olive oil and za'atar
or fresh figs,
chopped pistachios
and honey

Serves 4–6 as a starter or side

Mix the yoghurt with the salt in a bowl.

Drape a large square of cheesecloth/muslin over a bowl and empty the yoghurt into the cloth (see the step-by-step pictures, overleaf). Bring up the corners to make a little Dick-Whittington-type parcel. Tie tightly and leave enough string to hang the parcel up, with the bowl underneath to catch the liquid that drips out. I hang mine from a kitchen cupboard, but you could hang it on the tap over the kitchen sink or simply put it in a strainer over a bowl.

Leave the yoghurt to drip overnight so it loses enough moisture to become a soft cheese. Squeeze the bag to get more liquid out. You will be thrilled with the outcome and be able to call yourself a cheese-maker.

Once it has the consistency of a thick cream cheese, transfer to a small serving bowl. Drizzle with olive oil and za'atar, or top with sliced figs, chopped pistachios and honey.

3

5

6

Fava Dip

Lennie I first tried fava dip on Limnonari beach in the Greek island of Skopelos a few years ago and I don't know why it had taken me so long to discover it. Fava is an authentic Greek dip made from yellow split peas. It's less well known than hummus and thinner in texture but equally delicious. Serve with flatbread or Pitta Chips (page 28). You can grill some squid and put it on top, add some chopped anchovies, onion and capers, or – if you are brave and really trying to be Greek – serve with grilled octopus, which you can make yourself or may find available in Mediterranean delis.

250g yellow split peas

1 large onion, roughly chopped

2 garlic cloves, crushed

1 bay leaf

2 tbsp lemon juice

1 tbsp good-quality extra virgin olive oil

½–1 tsp mild (sweet) paprika

2 tbsp capers, to serve

salt and pepper

Serves 6–8

Rinse the split peas thoroughly. Put them in a pan, add cold water to cover the peas by 2–3cm and bring to the boil. Drain and rinse under cold water to remove any scum.

Return to the pan and add about 700ml fresh cold water (double the volume of the split peas), then add the onion, garlic, bay leaf and plenty of salt and pepper. Bring to the boil, then simmer over a moderate heat for 30–45 minutes until the split peas are soft (check the packet cooking times). Keep an eye on the pan to ensure it doesn't boil dry – you may need to top up with a little more boiling water. When the peas are cooked, strain off any remaining liquid and remove the bay leaf.

Whizz the peas in a blender or food processor with the lemon juice, olive oil and paprika. Taste and adjust the seasoning. Add a little water if it is too thick: the consistency should be thinner than hummus and it will become firmer as it cools.

Serve at room temperature with the capers on top.

Chris
mukkah

Jessie **'Chrismukkah'** is a term coined by *The O.C.*'s darling Seth Cohen – a character in the American TV drama. It's a coming together of Judaism and Christianity over the festive period. Basically, you can get the Chanukah gelt but still have something to open on the 25th December. Thank Jesus for Seth.

My husband has never understood why I'm indifferent to staying in the UK over Christmas. In his head, it snows every year, chestnuts are *always* roasting on an open fire and there's never a family rift. The constant struggle to persuade him to leave a snowless Blighty for a hot winter holiday is almost grounds for divorce.

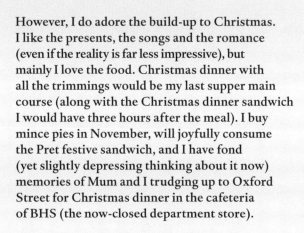

However, I do adore the build-up to Christmas. I like the presents, the songs and the romance (even if the reality is far less impressive), but mainly I love the food. Christmas dinner with all the trimmings would be my last supper main course (along with the Christmas dinner sandwich I would have three hours after the meal). I buy mince pies in November, will joyfully consume the Pret festive sandwich, and I have fond (yet slightly depressing thinking about it now) memories of Mum and I trudging up to Oxford Street for Christmas dinner in the cafeteria of BHS (the now-closed department store).

Yes, I'm Jewish, but was lucky enough to have a Goy (non-Jewish) father, which meant that we had Chanukah 'gelt' (money, in both real and chocolate form) from my mum's side but never missed a Christmas. And I was clever enough to marry out to a man whose family take Christmas *very* seriously.

So, here are some of our favourite recipes that revolve around the festive period, along with some unorthodox extras from my travels along the way. These can work for any festive celebration really, they are just some solid family faves... perhaps I shall try them for next year's 'Eastover'?

Lennie **I absolutely love Christmas dinner** and although I moan about the work involved, I really enjoy eating the food. I have memories of the children devouring too much chocolate from their stockings and zooming around the house all morning playing with their new (invariably noisy) toys.

Do you have lunch or dinner? I always prefer lunch, but later than normal to allow for our traditional smoked salmon and scrambled egg breakfast to go down. So, around 3pm on a darkening Christmas afternoon is perfect for us to enjoy our meal. A bit later, we'll be sitting on the sofa watching Christmas telly, with a large Baileys and a Christmas sandwich.

Devilled Eggs

Lennie   I heard on Radio 4 a long discussion about the origins of devilled eggs. In the eighteenth century, 'devilling' was used for meat, seafood and even bones, as well as eggs. This seems very retro, but Jessie tells me it's all the go now. If you do not want to use the spicy Tabasco and cayenne pepper, you could use a teaspoon of curry powder instead.

Jessie   I have an issue with anyone else making egg mayonnaise for me. So I guess I will be in charge of these over the festive period!

12 large free-range eggs,
at room temperature

4 tbsp mayonnaise

1–2 tsp Dijon mustard

1 tsp salt

¼ tsp cayenne pepper,
plus extra for sprinkling

few drops of Tabasco sauce

2 tbsp olive oil

2–3 tbsp freshly boiled water
(optional)

2 tsp snipped fresh chives

Serves 8

Put the eggs in a large pan of cold water, set over a high heat and bring to the boil. Simmer for 4 minutes, then turn off the heat and leave them in the water for 12 minutes. Transfer the eggs to a bowl of cold water and leave for about 15 minutes before you peel them.

Peel the eggs and cut in half lengthways. Take out the yolks and put them in a bowl. Add the mayonnaise, mustard, salt, cayenne and a few drops of Tabasco and mash together using the back of a fork. Add a little olive oil, then use a stick blender to blend until smooth. Taste and adjust the seasoning. If the mixture seems thick, stir in a little freshly boiled water.

Place the egg white halves on a serving plate. Either spoon the egg yolk mixture into the whites, or pipe it in. Sprinkle with cayenne and chives, then serve.

Beetroot and Gin-Cured Salmon

Lennie **Probably the longest prep time of any recipe: two days! Really easy though, although confidence and a gin and tonic might assist.**

piece of salmon from
the thick end (about 800g),
skinned

fresh dill, to garnish (optional)

BEETROOT CURE
300g beetroot, peeled and
roughly chopped

300g demerara sugar

300g table salt

1 tsp black peppercorns

2 tsp juniper berries,
crushed

grated zest and juice
of 3 limes

grated zest and juice
of 1 orange

200ml gin

3 tbsp wholegrain mustard

1 star anise

Serves 8

To make the cure, whizz the beetroot, sugar, salt, peppercorns and juniper in a food processor until puréed. Add the lime and orange zest and juice, along with the gin and mustard, and whizz again.

Pour half of the cure mixture into a container large enough to hold the fish, add the star anise, then lay the salmon on top and pour over the remaining cure. Cover and chill overnight.

The next day, remove the salmon and give the cure a good stir. Put the salmon back, ensuring it's submerged in the cure, cover and chill for a further 24 hours.

To serve, rinse the salmon under cold running water and discard the cure. Slice the salmon into 3–5mm thick slices and serve on buttered rye or pumpernickel bread, with a little fresh dill scattered over if you like.

Gorgonzola, Fig and Walnut Tartlets

Lennie   **Embarrassingly easy, if you use ready-made mini tartlet cases or croustades! If you can't find fresh figs, you could use six chopped dried figs instead.**

24 ready-made mini tartlet
cases or croustades

50g walnuts, chopped

150g Gorgonzola or other
blue cheese, chopped

4 fresh figs, chopped
or sliced

fresh cranberries,
to garnish (optional)

Makes 24

Preheat the oven to 200°C/180°C fan/gas 6.

Arrange the tartlet cases on a baking sheet. Add a few chopped walnuts to each tartlet case, then add a heaped teaspoon of Gorgonzola and top with a chunk of fig.

Bake for 5–10 minutes until the cheese melts. Serve warm, garnished with fresh cranberries if you like.

See picture on the following page.

Brie and Cranberry Parcels

Lennie   I made these up one Christmas because of the cranberry sauce
that's everywhere. It goes so well with Brie and the little tartlets
are delicious. If you prefer, you can make these into even smaller
single-bite-size parcels: cut the pastry into 12cm squares, reduce the
amount of filling slightly and twist the tops to seal before baking.

50g unsalted butter, melted,
for brushing

250–270g pack of filo pastry

150g Brie, cut into 2cm cubes

60g cranberry sauce

Makes 10

Preheat the oven to 200°C/180°C fan/gas 6. Lightly brush 10 holes
of a cupcake tin with a little of the melted butter.

Cut the filo pastry sheets into approximately 15cm squares. Stack them
up and cover with a damp clean tea towel to prevent them drying out
while you work.

Take a square of filo, brush with melted butter and place into a hole of
the cupcake tin. Repeat with 2 more squares of pastry, brushing each
one with butter and placing it at a slight angle on top of the square in
the tin to form a star shape. Repeat with all the pastry squares until you
have 10 pastry cases in the tin.

Fill the middle of each pastry case with a few cubes of Brie and a
teaspoon of cranberry sauce. Bring all the edges of the pastry together
to form a pouch and pinch hard at the neck to seal. Brush with the
remaining melted butter and bake for 10 minutes until golden and crisp.

Leave to cool in the tin for a few minutes before serving.

See picture on the following page.

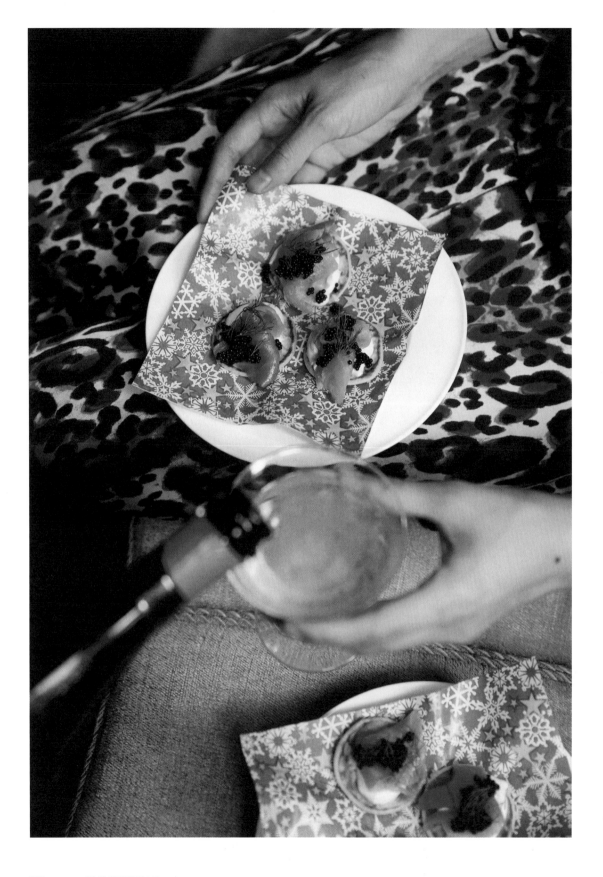

Blinis with Horseradish Cream and Smoked Salmon

Lennie **Sooooo easy – it's not worth buying the ready-made ones. The blinis can be made the night before you want to serve them: store in an airtight container in the fridge. A fabulous appetiser.**

1 large egg

150ml milk

25g unsalted butter, melted

100g plain flour

pinch of fine salt

vegetable oil, for frying

TOPPING

180g crème fraîche

3–4 tbsp creamed horseradish

smoked salmon

lumpfish roe (optional)

fresh dill (optional)

Makes about 40

To make the topping, mix the crème fraîche with the horseradish. Cover and leave in the fridge.

In a jug, whisk together the egg, milk and melted butter. Sift the flour and salt into a bowl and make a well in the centre. Slowly pour the milk mixture into the centre, stirring constantly and gradually bringing in the flour from the sides until you have a smooth batter.

Brush a large frying pan or griddle with oil and heat to a moderate temperature. Spoon a dessertspoon of the batter onto the pan to form a round shape, about 3.5cm in diameter. You should be able to cook 5 or 6 blinis at a time. Cook for 2–3 minutes until the mixture is dry on top, then flip over and cook the other side for 2–3 minutes – both sides should be nicely golden. Drain on kitchen paper while you cook the remaining blinis. Leave to cool completely before adding the topping.

Spread a teaspoon of the horseradish cream on each blini and then top with a sliver of smoked salmon and, if you like, a little lumpfish roe (pretend caviar) and a few dill fronds.

Quick and Easy Chicken Liver Pâté

Jessie

This is a recipe from my dearest cousin Sarah: the best bubble-bath blower, the funnest cousin and also the queen of a chicken liver pâté. A Christmas family favourite, this is really easy but is best made the day before you need it so it can set properly.

250g chicken livers, thoroughly defrosted if frozen

200g unsalted butter

1 onion, roughly chopped

2 garlic cloves, chopped

2 large eggs, lightly beaten

2–3 tablespoons amontillado sherry

salt and pepper

Serves 6–8

Rinse the livers under cold water and cut out any gristle, excess fat or green bits. Dry them thoroughly on kitchen paper: any excess water will make the mixture too wet.

Melt 125g of the butter in a heavy-based frying pan, add the onion and garlic and cook over a low heat for about 15 minutes until the onion is soft. Add the chicken livers and fry over a low heat, turning frequently, until the livers are firm but still slightly pink in the middle.

Pour the eggs into the pan and leave to cook until just set over the liver and onion mixture. Turn off the heat and let everything cool for at least 15 minutes.

Tip the mixture into a food processor along with the sherry and add 10 grindings of salt and 5 grindings of black pepper. Pulse until smooth. Taste and adjust the seasoning. The consistency should be slightly runny: it will firm up as it cools. If it seems too dry, add another spoonful of sherry. Pour into a container with a tight-fitting lid and chill for 30 minutes.

Meanwhile, gently melt the remaining 75g butter in a small saucepan, skimming off any skum. Spoon the melted butter over the top of the pâté to form a thin layer (this will stop the pâté from discolouring), then return the container to the fridge to chill overnight.

Serve with melba toasts, warm fresh toast or crackers.

Stilton, Red Onion, Apple and Walnut Tart

Lennie

These classic flavours create a beautiful festive tart to serve up at the Christmas dinner table. It looks great, tastes delicious and is so easy to make.

1 sheet ready-rolled all-butter puff pastry (about 320g)

25g unsalted butter

3 red onions, thinly sliced

1 tbsp light soft brown sugar

1 tbsp red wine vinegar

2 heaped tbsp red onion chutney (or any other chutney for cheese)

1 Braeburn or Gala apple, cored and cut into thin segments

150g Stilton or other blue cheese, crumbled

75g walnut pieces

10 fresh thyme sprigs

salt

Serves 6

Preheat the oven to 200°C/180°C fan/gas 6 and place a large baking sheet inside to heat up.

Unroll the pastry sheet and place on a large piece of baking parchment. Using a sharp knife, score a 2cm border around the edges, taking care not to cut completely through the pastry. Using a fork, prick the pastry all over inside the border. Transfer the pastry – on the parchment – to the hot baking sheet and bake for about 15 minutes until lightly golden all over.

Meanwhile, heat the butter in a large heavy-based frying pan, add the onions and a good pinch of salt and fry for about 10 minutes until soft. Add the sugar and vinegar and stir until heated through and the sugar has dissolved. Set aside.

Remove the pastry from the oven and gently press down the centre with the back of a fork. Spread the chutney over the pastry, then cover with the onions, keeping within the border. Arrange the apple segments over the onions, then add the crumbled Stilton and walnuts, and scatter the thyme on top. Return to the oven for 15 minutes until the cheese is bubbling and the pastry is golden brown.

Leave to cool for at least 5 minutes before slicing. It's also lovely served at room temperature.

Jansson's Temptation

Jessie Ragnhild, my husband's godmother (if agnostic socialists who lived in a feminist commune have such a title for their dearest friends), is a wonderful cook. She just couldn't stay away from my mother-in-law Tessa after their Brixton commune days, so she found a house next door to her, with a direct passage to each other's kitchen. One day, she passed this beloved Swedish winter classic over the garden wall. It is fundamentally a creamy potato gratin with fish. Ragnhild likes to make this with Swedish sprats, which confusingly are often sold with the word 'ansjovis' on the tin – but they are not the same as Mediterranean anchovies and have a milder, less salty flavour. We English philistines usually use anchovies. Don't be put off by the anchovies – they melt away, but add such wonderful flavour. Perfect comfort food.

25g unsalted butter, plus extra for greasing

3 large white onions, finely sliced into rings

1kg potatoes

50g tin anchovy fillets, drained and halved

300ml double cream

150ml whole milk

small handful of crumbled crispbread or dried breadcrumbs

Serves 8

Preheat the oven to 190°C/170°C fan/gas 5.

Heat the butter in a large heavy-based pan, add the onions and fry over a low heat for 15–20 minutes until soft and caramelised.

Meanwhile, peel the potatoes and cut into slim chip shapes, about 1–2cm wide.

Butter a baking dish (about 1.5–2 litres capacity). Layer the potatoes and onions in the dish, adding the anchovies among the layers.

Mix the cream and milk and pour over the potatoes: they should be almost covered. Scatter the crispbread or breadcrumbs over the top.

Cover with foil and bake for 50 minutes, then remove the foil and bake for a further 10 minutes. Serve hot.

Tip White onions are better in terms of the appearance of this dish, although it doesn't really matter.

Roast Turkey with Two Stuffings

Lennie

We never had sausagemeat when I was growing up because we didn't eat pork. So my mum and my sister always made what they called 'forcemeat', with minced beef. I still do this and everyone loves it with the turkey dinner at Christmas. I also make an apricot and nut stuffing, which we all adore – it's great cooked separately too, as a side for vegetarians. Add more of everything if you've got a huge turkey.

4.5–5kg turkey

50g unsalted butter

salt and pepper

MEAT STUFFING

1 onion, peeled

500g minced beef (not too lean as a little fat helps the turkey stay moist)

100g dried or fresh cranberries

25g unsalted butter

small handful each of fresh sage, rosemary and thyme leaves, chopped

1 bay leaf

APRICOT AND WALNUT STUFFING

1 onion, peeled

4 thick slices of bread, preferably wholemeal

165g dried apricots, chopped

150g walnut halves (or chestnuts)

50g unsalted butter

small handful each of fresh sage, rosemary and thyme leaves, chopped

grated zest of 1 orange

GRAVY

cooking juices from the bird (see method)

2 tbsp plain flour

1 glass dry white wine

500ml chicken or turkey stock

Serves 10–12

Preheat the oven to 200°C/180°C fan/gas 6.

For the meat stuffing: put the onion into a food processor and roughly chop. Add the minced beef, cranberries, butter, chopped herbs and a good seasoning of salt and pepper and whizz briefly, just to combine. Use this to stuff the neck end of the turkey, pushing the bay leaf into the stuffing, and pull the skin over to enclose, securing with a few toothpicks.

For the apricot and walnut stuffing: put the onion into the food processor and chop, add the bread and chop again. Add the apricots, walnuts, butter, herbs, orange zest and a good seasoning of salt and pepper and whizz again. The mixture should be quite sticky and moist (add more butter if not). Stuff the cavity of the turkey with this mixture.

Weigh the turkey and make a note of the weight including the stuffing, then put the bird in a roasting tin. Spread the butter over the turkey and season with salt and pepper. Cover with foil and cook for about 4–4½ hours, depending on the amount of stuffing: allow 20 minutes per 500g. Remove the foil for the last 45 minutes to brown the bird.

Remove from the oven, place the turkey on a board, cover with foil and leave in a warm place to rest for 1 hour before carving.

To make the gravy: put the roasting tin with the cooking juices over a medium–high heat, stir the flour into the juices and cook for a few minutes, scraping up the bits from the bottom of the roasting tin with a wooden spoon. Add the white wine and bring to a rapid boil. Add the stock, bring back to the boil and then strain into a saucepan. Place back over the heat and simmer for another 5–10 minutes until slightly thickened.

To serve, carve the turkey. Slice the meat stuffing and serve with the turkey, with spoonfuls of the apricot stuffing and the gravy on the side.

Bread Sauce

Jessie   So easy peasy. My brother Alex would eat this on its own or in a sandwich. It's obligatory with roast turkey at Christmas and is great with roast chicken.

12 whole cloves

1 whole white onion, peeled

600ml whole milk

20g unsalted butter

4 thick slices of white bread, crusts removed (about 100g), whizzed into breadcrumbs

a good grating of fresh nutmeg or ½ tsp ground nutmeg (optional)

salt and pepper

Serves 10–12

Push the cloves into the onion. Place the onion in a pan with the milk and butter and slowly bring to the boil over a low heat. Turn off the heat and leave the milk to infuse for a couple of hours.

Remove the onion and cloves and add the breadcrumbs, stirring over a low heat until the sauce thickens. Add salt and pepper, and nutmeg (if using), to taste.

Serve hot.

Roasted Brussels Sprouts with Grapes and Hazelnuts

Jessie   Even though we were all going to Goa the next morning, Mum thought it incredibly important to get a Christmas dinner in with the whole – already bickering – family. This was a bit of a kitchen smash-and-grab on my part, but the grapes, vinegar and hazelnuts work wonderfully to spruce up the trusty sprout and the roasting adds a sweetness that can convert any sprout-hater.

1kg Brussels sprouts, trimmed

220g seedless red grapes

2 tbsp olive oil

2 tbsp moscatel wine vinegar (or half balsamic, half sherry vinegar)

1 tbsp light soy sauce

1 tsp thyme leaves

75g hazelnuts, roughly chopped

pepper, to taste

Serves 8–10 as a side

Preheat the oven to 220°C/200°C fan/gas 7.

In a large roasting tin (you may need 2 tins), toss the Brussels sprouts and grapes with the olive oil, vinegar, soy sauce and thyme, and add some pepper. Spread them evenly in the tin and roast for 20 minutes, shaking the tin every so often so they cook evenly.

Add the hazelnuts and roast for another 15 minutes or until the sprouts and grapes are browned and blistered and the hazelnuts are a nice golden colour.

Serve hot.

Spiced Red Cabbage

Jessie   Mum's red cabbage is the smell of Christmas – and so delicious.
If you make too much, it freezes well and tastes great with all kinds
of meat. It's also great with Boxing Day leftovers.

Lennie   You can make this in the oven or on the hob: the oven will create
a slightly drier version, the stove will be a little more wet. You can
add a drop of port if you fancy and this makes it quite luxurious
at Christmas. You can make it a day or two in advance so there's
less to do on Christmas day and the aroma gets everyone in the
Christmas mood.

Serves 8–10 as a side

50g unsalted butter

1 large onion, sliced

1 red cabbage (white core
discarded), shredded

2 garlic cloves

1 or 2 cooking apples,
peeled and chopped
into pieces

about 10 whole cloves

1 tsp ground cinnamon

½ tsp caraway seeds
(optional)

2 tbsp red wine or cider vinegar

1 tbsp brown sugar

2–3 tbsp port (optional)

salt and pepper

Preheat the oven to 180°C/160°C fan/gas 4.

Heat the butter in a large flameproof casserole dish. Add the onion,
cabbage and garlic and sauté together for about 10 minutes.

Add the apples, cloves, cinnamon, caraway (if using), vinegar and
sugar and stir for a couple of minutes, then add 50ml water and the
port (if using). Cover with a lid and place in the oven – or simmer on
the hob – for about 1 hour, stirring halfway through, until the cabbage
is soft. Season to taste.

Serve hot.

Mum's Leftover Turkey Casserole

Jessie   I will never understand how people have enough leftover Christmas turkey to survive until the New Year. We usually have scraps the next day, just enough to make the Boxing Day 'everything but the kitchen sink' sandwich while we bet on a horse at Kempton Races. These people that are still dealing with their bird on the 28th must not be as greedy as my family.

This dish is by no means a sexy show-stopper, rather a nostalgic warmer and something my brother and I are always so happy to be greeted with at the table. It works with the turkey leftovers, but you should make it anytime you feel like being cheered up.

Lennie   I first made this dish using leftover turkey after Christmas, but everyone liked it so much that I began to cook it throughout the year. It is nourishing, wholesome and cheap.

500g turkey (leftover cooked turkey or fresh turkey breast steaks), chopped

25g plain flour, seasoned with salt and pepper

25g unsalted butter

2 leeks, sliced into 1cm rounds

5 carrots, chopped into slices

2 celery sticks, chopped into slices

500ml chicken stock

150g frozen peas

Serves 6–8

Preheat the oven to 180°C/160°C fan/gas 4.

In a large mixing bowl, toss the turkey with the seasoned flour to coat.

Heat the butter in a flameproof casserole dish, add the turkey and fry, turning from time to time, until it just starts to brown. Add the leeks, carrots, celery and stock, cover and cook in the oven for about 45 minutes. Add the frozen peas and return to the oven for 2–3 minutes to heat through.

Serve hot, with a jacket potato.

Roast Beef and Yorkshires

Lennie My son-in-law tells me my roasts are legendary, probably because they are my favourite meal. Admittedly, I can cook roast beef that will make everyone swoon. Sadly, my Yorkshires (page 228) never really make anyone swoon; they are often too soggy, flat or stick to the pan and you can't get them out, resembling a sad toad-in-the-hole without any of the sausage. My family are very tolerant and say they are delicious anyway. Buy the best joint you can afford. I think rolled sirloin or ribeye is the best, but expect to spend up to £60 for a piece – so this has got to be for your most favourite people.

Jessie I think Mum's Yorkshires are the accidental triumph of her roasts. Who wants thin pudding with loads of air when you can have a Yorkshire cake/friand?

2–2.5kg boneless rolled sirloin or rib-eye, removed from the fridge at least 1 hour before cooking to come to room temperature

8 shallots (or small onions), unpeeled

salt and pepper

YORKSHIRE PUDDINGS
see page 228 for recipe

GRAVY
350ml red wine

350ml beef or chicken stock

2 tbsp redcurrant jelly (optional)

Serves 8

Preheat the oven to 220°C/200°C fan/gas 7.

Season the meat with salt and pepper. Heat a heavy-based frying pan over a high heat, add the meat and sear the fat until browned all over.

Put the shallots in a roasting tin and sit the meat on top, fat-side up. Roast for 20 minutes, then turn the oven down to 160°C/140°C fan/gas 3 and roast for another 30 minutes (or 15 minutes per kilo) for medium rare. Reduce the cooking time by 10 minutes for rare or extend by 10 minutes for medium (and bear in mind that you might want to adjust timings depending on the shape of your joint – a long thin joint will need slightly less time than a thicker shorter joint). If you have a digital probe or meat thermometer, the internal temperature will be 50°C for rare beef.

(Meanwhile, start preparing your Yorkshires – see page 228.) Remove the beef from the oven, place on a carving board, cover loosely with foil and leave to rest for at least 30 minutes or up to an hour.

To make the gravy: put the roasting tin with the cooking juices over a medium–high heat and add the red wine, scraping up the bits from the bottom of the roasting tin with a wooden spoon. Add the stock and bring to a rapid boil. Turn the heat down slightly, add the redcurrant jelly, if using, and simmer until reduced and slightly thickened. Add the juices from the resting beef, stir well and season to taste.

To serve, carve the beef in thin slices and serve with your Yorkshires and gravy on the side.

Yorkshire Puddings

Lennie   **These *do* actually work – after 50 years of experimentation!**

3 large eggs

155g plain flour

200ml whole milk

4 tbsp sunflower oil

salt and pepper

Makes 8

Beat the eggs in a mixing bowl with some salt and pepper and then gradually add the flour, whisking it in with a balloon whisk. Add the milk a little at a time until all is combined. Leave to stand in the fridge for 30 minutes or until ready to use.

Preheat the oven to 200°C/180°C fan/gas 6 (or turn the heat up again while the beef is resting – see page 226). Put 1½ teaspoons of the oil in each of 8 holes of a 12-hole muffin tin and put the tin in the oven to heat up for at least 20 minutes.

Carefully pour the Yorkshire pudding batter evenly between the 8 oiled muffin holes and cook in the oven for about 30–35 minutes until risen and golden. Don't open the oven during cooking.

Serve immediately.

Puddings
and Bakes

Jessie My brother Alex is a doctor.

But you probably know this already as my mother tells anyone she meets. If she could have that batman signal shining over London with 'my son the doctor!', she would. In fact, in the reviews of the podcast, one comment said 'Love the podcast, but a little less about 'my son the doctor'. Quite rightly, she is extremely proud of him and having a singer and an actress in her other children pales in comparison. Never have I seen my mum move so fast as when over an aeroplane tannoy came the words she longed to hear most: 'Is there a doctor on board?' Yes, he saves lives, he is selfless, but he can't give me a prescription and whenever I'm ill and ask for assistance, he grunts 'I am sure you'll be fine.' What I'm most appreciative of is his methodical approach to baking and perfect presentation, something I have no patience for.

We would find him, aged seven, hosting tea parties in the garden with our au pair, Donatella. Tracey Chapman would be playing out of the open French windows and he would have a spread on the table-clothed plastic table, napkins folded, pouring 'cocktails' into tea cups and being the host with the most.

The Bar mitzvah gift the whole family were most grateful for was *not* the generous portions of Jack Daniel's a school friend poured us at the party and the subsequential line of vomiting teens in the toilets, but instead the ice-cream maker from the much-loved British department store John Lewis. It still lives at my mum's…and so does Alex. Over the years, we have devoured lemon, coffee, praline-and-cream, macadamia-brittle, clotted-cream, Oreo and stem-ginger ice creams.

In this chapter are some more of Alex's creations, among other delicious puddings that can satisfy a sweet tooth, impress a crowd, soothe heartbreak and save some time.

Lennie Alex's attention to detail has saved many a meal and also ensures our table is a delight to look at before you sit down.

Unlike Jessie and me, he is calm in the kitchen, although as a perfectionist he has been known to make two of something to ensure he gets it right (for example the blackberry and custard tart for Nigella). He is an all-round great cook, but his cakes and desserts are legendary. If only he could prescribe these to all his patients!

Mum's Raspberry Trifle

Jessie This reminds me of my childhood and Sunday lunches full of friends and family. It's nothing fancy. I think that is what I love about it. And Mum has never updated the retro recipe to make it more refined. A guaranteed crowd-pleaser even if you have very sophisticated tastes. The deliciousness of the cream with the custard is unbeatable.

Lennie My family like it when the custard sets and becomes wobbly and jelly-like. I would only use frozen fruits if I couldn't find tinned raspberries.

2 × 300g tins raspberries or 500g frozen summer fruits

1½ tbsp sugar (plus an extra 1½ tbsp if using frozen fruits)

2 raspberry Swiss rolls (190g each) with jam filling (no cream)

3–4 tbsp sweet sherry (optional)

2 tbsp custard powder

570ml whole milk

500ml double cream

handful of flaked almonds, to decorate

fresh raspberries, to decorate (optional)

Serves 8

If using frozen fruits, put them in a pan with 50ml water and 1½ tablespoons of sugar and heat gently until defrosted. Leave to cool.

Slice the Swiss rolls into 3cm slices and arrange attractively in the base of a round glass serving bowl.

Spoon the tinned raspberries (or cooled fruits) over the Swiss rolls, allowing the juice to soak into the sponge. If using tinned raspberries, add a dash or two of sherry, if you like.

Make the custard by mixing the custard powder and the sugar in a bowl with a little of the milk to create a paste. Heat the remaining milk in a pan over a low heat until it comes to the boil, then slowly add it to the custard paste and mix together. If you want a thicker custard, add more powder.

Pour the custard over the sponge and raspberries and leave to go cold.

Whip the cream until it forms soft peaks, but don't over-whip: it should be light. Spread the whipped cream over the custard. Sprinkle the almonds (you can lightly toast them in a pan if you want, but I never do) over the top and add a few fresh raspberries if you have them. Chill in the fridge for a couple of hours before serving.

Chocolate Mousse Tart

Lennie

This combines two delights: chocolate mousse and a buttery biscuit base. You could always just do the chocolate mousse if you didn't fancy the base: the olive oil is the added ingredient that works surprisingly well.

BISCUIT BASE

50g dark chocolate, broken up

50g unsalted butter, plus extra for greasing

2 tbsp cocoa powder, sifted

175g digestive biscuits

CHOCOLATE MOUSSE

150g dark chocolate, broken up

4 tbsp extra virgin olive oil

1 tsp instant coffee granules

4 large eggs, separated

2 tbsp caster sugar

1 tsp vanilla extract

Serves 8

Butter a 20cm springform tin and line the base and side with baking parchment.

For the biscuit base, melt the chocolate, butter and cocoa in a heatproof bowl over a pan of barely simmering water, stirring occasionally until melted and smooth.

Whizz the digestives in a food processor until they are reduced to fine crumbs. Add to the melted chocolate and mix until evenly distributed. Tip into the lined tin and use the back of a spoon to press firmly into the base and just up the side. Chill in the fridge.

For the chocolate mousse, melt the chocolate in a heatproof bowl over a pan of barely simmering water, stirring occasionally until smooth. Set aside to cool for 10 minutes, then stir in the olive oil.

Dissolve the coffee in a small splash of boiling water to make a paste, then stir into the chocolate mixture until well combined.

In a large bowl, whisk the egg yolks, sugar and vanilla together until pale and thick and doubled in volume. Carefully pour in the chocolate mixture and fold it into the yolk mixture until well combined.

In a separate spotlessly clean bowl, whisk the egg whites to firm peaks. Gently fold the whites into the chocolate mixture and then pour into the biscuit base. Chill for at least 4 hours until firm, or preferably overnight, before removing the springform tin. Serve chilled.

Cointreau Oranges

Jessie **This reminds me of Mum hosting a load of my father's work friends and us sneaking downstairs to catch a glimpse of who was joining the table. It all seemed rather glamorous. Although I was never a fan of this recipe as a child, I have somewhat of an affinity for it, and I feel it's been a little neglected recently, lost to millennial 'clean' or deconstructed desserts. So I thought this nostalgic dish deserved a place in the book, not only as a warm reminder of 1990s dinner parties, but also as a light yet robust boozy dessert.**

225g sugar

150ml Cointreau

6 oranges

Serves 6

Put the sugar into a pan, add 100ml water and place over a very low heat until the sugar has dissolved, agitating slightly with the handle of a wooden spoon to ensure it doesn't cake on the bottom of the pan, but do not stir. Using a pastry brush dipped in water, brush any sugar crystals down from the sides of the pan. Once all the sugar has dissolved, turn the heat up slightly and cook until it starts to caramelise. Do not stir – you can swirl the pan to move it about.

When the caramel reaches the desired light brown colour, remove it from the heat and add another 100ml water and the Cointreau (it will bubble up and spit a little): this will stop the cooking process. Leave to cool.

Using a sharp knife, peel the oranges, ensuring you also cut away the white pith. Shred the orange peel without the pith. Blanche in boiling water for 30 seconds then add later to the caramel. Cut the peeled oranges into 1cm slices and put into a glass serving bowl.

Once the caramel has cooled, pour over the oranges, then chill for at least 2 hours or overnight.

Serve as they are or with slightly sweetened whipped cream and grated dark chocolate if you wish.

'Ode to Nora' Key Lime Pie

Lennie

This is our tribute to the wonderful Nora Ephron, whose Key lime pie was renowned in her brilliant book *Heartburn*. 'If there is a Nora Ephron signature anything it is that there's slightly too much food.' A woman after our own heart. Celebrate with this pie; throw it in someone's face who has broken your heart; or eat it all by yourself.

300g Hobnobs

100g unsalted butter, melted

4 large egg yolks

397g tin condensed milk

150ml double cream, plus 150ml extra, whipped, to decorate (optional)

finely grated zest and juice of 6 limes

Serves 6

Preheat the oven to 180°C/160°C fan/gas 4.

Crush the biscuits into crumbs (either pulse in a food processor or place in a large food bag, seal and then roll or bash with a rolling pin), then transfer to a bowl and stir in the melted butter.

Tip the crumb mixture into a 20cm springform tin and use the back of a spoon to press evenly into the base and up the side. Bake for 10 minutes and then leave to cool.

In a large bowl, whisk the egg yolks until light, then whisk in the condensed milk until smooth (on the slowest speed if using an electric whisk). Add the cream, lime juice and zest (reserving the zest of one of the limes to decorate) and whisk until slightly thickened.

Tip the filling mixture into the biscuit base and bake for 12–15 minutes until just set on top but still slightly wobbly. Leave to cool, then chill for at least 4 hours, or preferably overnight, until firm.

To serve, remove the springform tin and decorate the pie with whipped cream and a little lime zest. Alternatively, just serve with crème fraîche.

Tropical Fruit Salad

Jessie

I may have overdone this recipe in my house as I distinctly remember my husband saying 'we're not having that bloody tropical fruit salad again, are we?' But it's because it's a gem! My mum's beautiful cousin Liz made this once when we were visiting, because there is nothing like a 'tropical' fruit salad to brighten up a grey Mancunian day. I'm not a pudding-maker so this works for me – it's fresh, tasty and quick, and it tastes even better the next day as the stem ginger and fruit juices blend together. Make a load of it and keep it in the fridge for a few days.

1 pineapple, peeled, cored and roughly diced (2–3cm chunks)

2 mangoes, peeled and chopped or sliced

2 papayas, peeled, seeded and chopped

2 oranges, peeled and segmented or sliced

4 kiwi fruit, peeled and sliced

400g tin lychees

4 balls of stem ginger from a jar, finely chopped

chopped fresh mint, to serve (optional)

Serves 8

Put all of the fresh fruit into a large serving bowl or layer attractively on a large platter.

Add the lychees, juice and all. Add the chopped ginger (and a teaspoon of the syrup from the jar if you like). Gently mix together.

Serve with crème fraîche or yoghurt, and a sprinkling of chopped mint, if using.

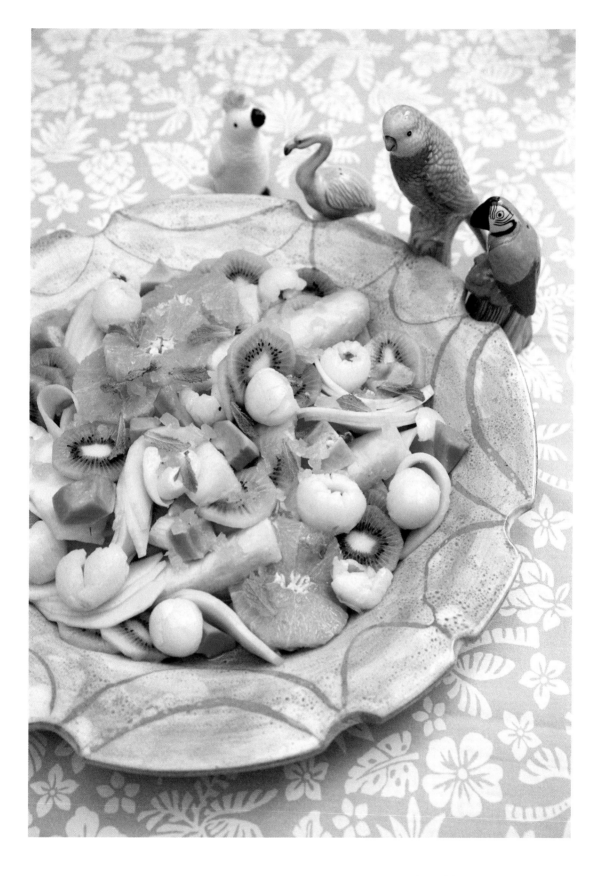

Passionate Eton Mess

Jessie   We made this for our guest Deborah Frances-White, *The Guilty Feminist* podcaster, who was literally sticking her fingers in this pud while we asked her: 'Do you have good table manners?' The yoghurt really lightens it up compared to the usual Eton mess.

Lennie   A dish that ardent feminists can't resist. Well, the guilty ones at least. An unadulterated objectified dessert.

300ml double cream

200ml Greek yoghurt

3–4 meringue nests, lightly crushed

2 passion fruits, cut in half and pulp scooped out

400g raspberries

50g coconut flakes, toasted

Serves 6

Whip the cream until stiff, then stir in the yoghurt. Keep in the fridge until ready to serve.

Fold the meringue, passion fruit pulp and raspberries into the cream mixture. Transfer to a serving bowl and top with toasted coconut.

Griddled Peaches with Rosemary and Honeyed Greek Yoghurt

Jessie

A peach is not a peach unless you eat it under the Greek sun, among the chirping crickets and with thick Greek yoghurt and Skopelos honey. However, Dalston will have to do. This is an easy pudding that makes supermarket peaches that bit more tasty and the rosemary adds a lovely aromatic touch.

6 peaches, halved
and stoned

1 tbsp demerara sugar

about 20g unsalted butter

3 sprigs of rosemary

2–3 tbsp clear honey

500g good Greek yoghurt

flaked almonds (optional),
toasted

Serves 6

Heat a griddle pan over a medium heat. If you don't have a griddle pan, use a frying pan.

Sprinkle the flat fleshy half of each peach with a tiny bit of sugar to help them caramelise.

Add the butter and the sprigs of rosemary to the hot pan. Place the peaches flat-side down on the griddle, cook for 4 minutes then turn one of them over to check how they're doing. You should see lovely black griddle lines (if you don't, then cook for a little longer on a higher heat). Turn all the peaches over and cook for a further 4 minutes.

While they are cooking, stir some honey into the Greek yoghurt.

Take the peaches off the heat and serve with a dollop of honeyed Greek yoghurt, scattering some toasted flaked almonds over the top.

See picture on the following page.

Vera Sequira's Chocolate and Rum Pudding

Jessie While we were at our favourite place in Goa one Christmas, we tried this beautifully dense and boozy banger of a dessert. It is a recipe generously handed down by our friend Denzil, whose late mother Vera created the perfect alternative to a Christmas pudding. And you won't want to make it only at Christmastime. Denzil's mum used to set the pudding in a ring mould with vanilla ice cream dolloped in the middle. But it works in a loaf tin and is a great fridge cake. Alternatively, you could put the mixture into little ramekin pots. I love eating it cold, but it also tastes great at room temperature.

100g glacé cherries, chopped, plus extra to serve

100g walnuts, chopped, plus extra to serve

75ml dark rum

250g dark chocolate, chopped

250ml single cream

125g icing sugar

100g rich tea or Marie biscuits, crushed into rough crumbs

Serves 8–10

Put the cherries and 70g of the walnuts into a bowl, pour in 35ml of the rum and leave to soak overnight.

Line a 900g loaf tin with a strip of baking parchment.

Put the chocolate and cream into a heatproof bowl over a pan of barely simmering water and leave until the chocolate has melted. Stir gently to combine. Take off the heat, add the icing sugar and stir again. Leave to cool.

Add the crushed biscuits and stir to mix, then add the walnut and cherry mixture, then the remaining chopped walnuts and rum. Spoon the mixture into the prepared mould or tin, or into ramekins, and chill until set.

Turn out of the mould or loaf tin and cut into slices, or eat straight from the ramekins. If you like, scatter a few more cherries and walnuts over each slice, to decorate.

Lemon Ice Cream

Jessie **Food critic (and apparently my brother's 'idol') Jay Rayner had three portions of this, while Alex hid. It is sublime. Serve alone or with a robust biscuit such as biscotti or ginger snaps. Either way, you will assume the status of a demi-god to all those that you offer it to.**

3 lemons

180g caster sugar

pinch of salt

450ml double cream

Makes about 650ml

Finely grate the zest of 1 lemon and set aside. Squeeze the juice of all 3 lemons.

In a large mixing bowl combine the lemon juice, sugar and salt, then slowly add the cream while whisking: I use an electric whisk on a medium speed. Once you have added all the cream, continue to whisk for a couple of minutes until the mixture has thickened and is just holding its shape.

Add the lemon zest, then transfer the mixture to your ice-cream maker and churn. If you have a very unprofessional ice-cream maker, like I do, the mix may not become particularly solid by the end of churning. Do not worry. Transfer the mixture into a container (for example a 1-litre loaf tin), place in the freezer and give it a quick whisk every couple of hours until it is more set. It should be ready to eat after about 4 hours.

If you do not have an ice-cream maker, pour the custard and lemon zest mixture into a container, cover and freeze for an hour or so until it begins to freeze. Whisk thoroughly, then return to the freezer. Repeat this process two or three times until you have a smooth ice cream.

It's best to take this ice cream out of the freezer about 10–15 minutes before serving, so that it is soft, velvety and even more delicious.

No-Churn Cappuccino Ice Cream

Jessie We entirely agree with the chef and food writer Samin Nosrat: coffee ice cream reigns supreme. Why wait for coffee Häagen-Dazs to return to the local newsagents when you can make a better one, without an ice-cream maker, at home?! This is so moreish and delightfully easy.

10 Ferrero Rochers (or as many as you like)

4 tbsp instant coffee granules

3–4 tbsp hot water

600ml double cream

397g tin condensed milk

Makes about 1 litre

Put the Ferrero Rochers into a food bag, seal and then lightly bash with a rolling pin.

Put the coffee in a large mixing bowl. Add the hot water, a tablespoon at a time, until all the granules are dissolved. Add the cream and condensed milk and whisk until soft peaks form. Tip half of the cream mixture into a 1.5-litre loaf tin and add a layer of crushed Ferrero Rochers. Pour the remaining cream mixture over and finish with the remaining Ferrero Rochers on top.

Freeze until set, at least 6 hours or preferably overnight. Take the ice cream out of the freezer about 15 minutes before serving.

Stem Ginger Ice Cream

A luxurious ice cream that has a perfect fierceness to it with the chewy chunks of stem ginger. Delicious on its own or with sticky toffee pudding.

4 large egg yolks

75g caster sugar

800ml double cream

1 vanilla pod, slit lengthways and seeds scraped out, or 2 tsp vanilla bean paste or extract

6–8 balls of stem ginger, diced, plus 6 tbsp ginger syrup

Makes about 1 litre

In a large bowl, cream together the egg yolks and sugar until pale and fluffy.

In a pan, combine the cream and vanilla pod and seeds (or paste/extract) and bring to a simmer over a medium heat. Slowly pour the hot cream over the egg and sugar mix, stirring all the time. Rinse out the pan and return the mixture to the pan over a low heat, stirring constantly until it thickens enough to coat the back of a spoon, taking care not to let it get too hot or it will curdle.

Strain the custard into a bowl, removing the vanilla pod if used, and set aside to cool: ideally it should be chilled for a good couple of hours before churning.

Once cooled, churn in an ice-cream maker. When you have 5 minutes left to churn, add the diced ginger and syrup. Transfer to a container and freeze.

If you do not have an ice-cream maker, put the custard, ginger and syrup into a container, cover and freeze for an hour or so until the mixture begins to freeze. Whisk thoroughly, then return to the freezer. Repeat this process two or three times until you have a smooth ice cream.

Take the ice cream out of the freezer about 15 minutes before serving.

Medjool Date 'Ice Cream' Fingers

Jessie — These are my favourite, easy, sweet fix that live in the freezer and satisfy an ice cream urge when you may have run out. Make sure you stock up as one is not enough. They taste like Snickers ice cream bars. Kids love them and it fools toddlers into thinking they have had an afternoon ice cream. I love almond butter in mine but my husband likes peanut butter. Take your pick!

12–16 Medjool dates

jar of nut butter, such as almond, peanut or cashew

sea salt flakes (optional)

Makes 12–16

Slice the dates in half lengthways, remove the stones and open up the dates like hotdog buns.

Spread a generous amount of nut butter in the groove in each date and sprinkle with a few sea salt flakes, if liked.

If you have a long, shallow freezerproof container, put all the dates in one layer and pop into the freezer. Alternatively, use a smaller deeper container and separate the layers with baking parchment otherwise the dates will stick together (not the end of the world as then you have to eat three at once).

Put in the freezer and leave for 2 hours until hardened. Eat immediately once out of the freezer (or if they have been in the freezer for more than 2 hours, take them out 5–10 minutes before eating).

Panettone Bread and Butter Pudding

Jessie I'm always very happy to receive a panettone from someone as a Christmas present. It's like a scented candle; it's not something you necessarily want to buy for yourself but you always gladly end up with too many by January. Here's an option if you want to use up one of those cakes. This recipe is so easy and works all year round, and you could use hot cross buns instead of panettone.

25g unsalted butter, plus extra for greasing

1 panettone (about 700g), sliced about 2cm thick

4 large eggs

3 tbsp caster sugar

450ml milk

450ml double cream, plus extra to serve

1½ tsp vanilla extract

Serves 8–10

Butter a large baking dish (about 1.5–2 litres capacity). Arrange the panettone slices in the baking dish in an overlapping layer – you might need to cut some in half.

Whisk the eggs, sugar, milk, cream and vanilla together and then pour over the panettone, ensuring it is all covered. Leave to soak for about 1 hour.

Preheat the oven to 180°C/160°C fan/gas 4.

Dot the surface of the panettone with the butter. Place the baking dish in a roasting tin and pour in about 3cm of just-boiled water around the baking dish. Bake for about 35 minutes until golden brown on top.

Serve with extra cream to pour over.

Rum Raisin Crème Brûlée

Jessie   We first had this in the Old Bailey. We weren't on trial but had been invited by a judge (an old Manchester friend of Mum's) to join him for one of their formal ceremonial lunches. We were surrounded by wigs, *Game of Thrones* fur capes, the Black Rod and brilliant conversation. A rum raisin crème brûlée was offered up, which none of the judges accepted (they went for the cheeseboard and fruit) but I happily wolfed down, all seven months pregnant and desperate for any booze.

When we went to make crème brûlée for actress Hayley Squires, we made literal flames.

Lennie   This recipe caused Jessie and I to have a culinary dispute, which is quite normal. Jessie was too handy with the blowtorch that was extremely fierce and not well attached. It was like arch chaos in the kitchen with flame throwers, setting fire to the crème brûlées. I had to take over, with disastrous results, and it was nearly mama brûlée – but we all laughed until we could not breathe.

Jessie   We felt this needed to be included in the book as a motivation to all new cooks: 'If at first you don't succeed, dust yourself off and try again' (if you haven't set fire to yourself).

Makes 4

50g raisins

2 tbsp white rum

300ml double cream

1 vanilla pod, slit lengthways and seeds scraped out

3 large egg yolks

50g caster sugar

4 tsp demerara sugar

The day before you want to serve this, soak the raisins in the rum overnight until lovely and plump.

Preheat the oven to 170°C/150°C fan/gas 3.

Divide the rum-soaked raisins between 4 × 150ml ramekin dishes.

Put the cream in a pan and add the vanilla pod and seeds. Place over a low heat until just below boiling point, then carefully fish out and discard the vanilla pod.

Meanwhile, whisk the egg yolks with the caster sugar. Slowly pour in the hot cream, whisking as you go.

Place the ramekins in a roasting tin and pour the custard into the ramekins. Pour boiling water into the roasting tin until it reaches two-thirds of the way up the sides of the ramekins. Bake for 25–30 minutes until just set but still wobbly.

Leave to cool and then chill for at least 3–4 hours or preferably overnight.

Sprinkle a teaspoon of demerara sugar over each ramekin and blowtorch until the sugar begins to sizzle and brown, but try not to set it on fire! If you don't have a blowtorch, preheat the grill to its highest setting. Pop the ramekins under the hot grill for 4–5 minutes to caramelise the sugar. Probably safer to be honest.

Chill the crème brûlées for at least 30 minutes before serving.

Alex's Orange Pistachio Cake

Jessie   My mother has forever said, 'I'm not a sweet-toothed person; give me a plate of cheese any day.' I have always related to this. But how come the first thing I do when I get through her door is march to the fridge, look on the top shelf and shove a handful of Revels or bite-size Twirls in my mouth? And how come the person that puts them on that shelf of guilt is my mother? She protests that it is all for my hardworking night-shifting brother Dr Alex, but you can't kid a kidder.

Alex feeds our 'reluctant' sweet addiction by dropping a cake like this in front of us and going off to work. It's fluffy and tangy and light and makes you think it's acceptable to have three slices. Cake solves so many things, apart from my postpartum waistline. This may even taste better the day after, so don't eat it all at once.

butter for greasing

200g unsalted
shelled pistachios

150g plain flour, sifted

1 tsp baking powder

4 large eggs

150g caster sugar

ORANGE SYRUP/PURÉE
4 clementines,
or 2 large oranges

150g brown sugar

150g caster sugar

2 tbsp orange blossom water
(optional)

Serves 10

Preheat the oven to 180°C/160°C fan/gas 4. Butter a 23cm springform cake tin.

First, make the orange syrup. Slice the clementines widthways into discs, with their skins on, as thinly as you can. Place in a pan with both of the sugars and 350ml water. Bring to the boil and simmer for 30–40 minutes. Add the orange blossom water, if using, then take the pan off the heat.

Select the best orange discs and place them in the cake tin. Strain off 150ml of the orange syrup and set aside. Using a hand blender, blend the remaining mixture (skins and all) to make a syrupy purée. Leave to cool.

To make the cake batter, blitz 150g of the pistachios in a food processor to a reasonably fine powder, speckled with a few chunky bits of pistachio. Mix with the sifted flour and baking powder, then set aside. Roughly chop the remaining pistachios.

Recipe continues on the following page.

Alex's Orange Pistachio Cake

In a large bowl, beat the eggs and caster sugar together with an electric whisk until you have a pale yellow mousse: this will take around 8 minutes. Gently fold in the cooled orange purée – do this with patience, you don't want to knock out the air. Now fold in the pistachio and flour mix. Again, be patient, gently folding until all is combined. Finally, add the roughly chopped pistachios and fold into the mix.

Transfer the mixture to the cake tin and bake for 45–50 minutes. It is done when a skewer or knife inserted into the centre comes out clean.

Leave the cake to cool in the tin for 15 minutes. Using a skewer, make multiple holes all over the cake, then pour over the reserved orange syrup. The holes will allow the syrup to soak through the cake. Leave the cake to fully cool and absorb the syrup.

When ready, place a serving plate on top of the cake tin, flip over, tap the top and release the sides of the tin. Those gorgeous orange discs become the crowning glory of this delicious cake. Serve with mascarpone or crème fraîche, if you like.

Chocolate Courgette Cake

Jessie This cake was made for the iconic Neneh Cherry when she came on the podcast. We had been told she was dairy free, my son was three weeks old and I demanded carbs and sugar. Mum made this gorgeous cake that was so airy you could forget you had already eaten two large wedges! It reminded me of Sara Lee bakes in the best possible way and is a great cake for any occasion.

Lennie So we had to make a dairy-free recipe. I thought this might be hard, but it wasn't. Jessie thought that I might even turn out to be a star baker; however, I don't think I will be appearing on *The Great British Bake Off* just yet. We couldn't resist adding a creamy topping here, but for Neneh Cherry I dusted it with icing sugar.

120ml sunflower oil, plus extra for greasing

3 large eggs

150g soft light brown sugar

150g plain flour

50g cocoa powder

1 tsp ground cinnamon

1 tsp baking powder

1 tsp bicarbonate of soda

½ tsp fine salt

200g courgette (1 medium–large courgette), grated

75g walnuts, roughly chopped

raspberries, to decorate (optional)

CHOCOLATE SOURED CREAM GANACHE (OPTIONAL IF DAIRY-FREE)

125g soured cream

100g dark chocolate (minimum 60 per cent cocoa solids), chopped

2 tsp icing sugar

pinch of salt

Serves 10

Preheat the oven to 180°C/160°C fan/gas 4. Grease a 20cm loose-bottomed or springform cake tin and line with baking parchment.

In a large bowl, using an electric whisk, beat the eggs and sugar together for about 2–3 minutes until light and fluffy. Slowly whisk in the oil. Sift all the dry ingredients together, then beat into the mixture until just combined.

Using a spatula or large spoon, fold in the courgette and walnuts. Tip the mixture into the cake tin and bake for 40–45 minutes or until a skewer inserted into the centre comes out clean. Leave the tin on a wire rack until completely cold.

For the ganache (if using), put all the ingredients in a heatproof bowl over a pan of barely simmering water – making sure the base of the bowl doesn't touch the water – and leave to melt, stirring occasionally, until combined. (If it looks slightly split, then stir in 1 teaspoon of just-boiled water from the kettle.) Spread over the cooled cake and leave to set slightly before serving.

Scatter some raspberries over the top for a pop of colour.

Pistachio Scones with Macerated Strawberries and Mascarpone

Jessie

Afternoon tea is one of the things that brings me most joy, until I'm wired on Lapsang Souchong and Assam, have eaten too many coronation chicken sandwiches and polished off the entire pot of clotted cream on one scone... then I just feel a bit sick. Here is a lighter and fresher take on the classic afternoon scone, which means you can hopefully intake even more in an afternoon sitting.

60g unsalted butter, cubed, plus extra for greasing

60g unsalted shelled pistachios

200g self-raising flour, plus extra for dusting

1 tsp baking powder

40g caster sugar

100ml milk

1 tsp lemon juice

2 large eggs

mascarpone cheese, to serve

MACERATED STRAWBERRIES

400g strawberries

100g caster sugar

juice of 1 lime

Makes 8–10

Preheat the oven to 220°C/200°C fan/gas 7 and grease a baking sheet.

To make the macerated strawberries, thinly slice the strawberries and add to a bowl along with the caster sugar and lime juice. Mix well and set aside to allow time for them to turn into a delicious sticky mess.

To make the scones, blitz the pistachios in a food processor until you have a reasonably fine powder with the occasional chunk of nut. Sift the flour with the baking powder and mix with the pistachios and sugar. Add the cubed butter and rub together, using your fingertips, until you have a crumble-like texture.

Put the milk in a large mixing jug, add the lemon juice, then whisk together with the eggs. Slowly add this to the flour, mixing continuously: you may not need to add all of the milk mix – add just enough to get a sticky dough. Set aside any remaining milk mix to glaze the scones.

Turn the dough out onto a floured work surface and knead very briefly. Be generous with dusting with flour, otherwise the dough will stick to your hands. Roll out the dough to 2–3cm thick. Using a 6cm cutter, cut out the scones and place on the baking sheet. Bring the trimmed dough together to make a couple of extra scones. Brush the tops with the remaining milk and egg mix. Bake for about 10 minutes until risen and golden brown.

Serve warm from the oven, with the macerated strawberries and mascarpone.

Tip These are great when fresh out of the oven, but as soon as they have cooled down they are very crumbly. If they are kept for any length of time, you could reheat them before eating.

'Triple Threat' Chocolate Brownies

Jessie People have requested this recipe the most after hearing about it in the Ed Sheeran episode. A triple shot of chocolatey goodness, my doctor brother Alex says that it's more like a 'triple threat' to your cholesterol levels, but don't let that stop you from making them.

Get creative! Add whatever you like to your brownie batter. Generous chunks of white, milk or dark chocolate will all work well, as will roughly broken-up Oreos or any other chocolate confectionery. I generally add three things to mine, hence the triple threat. Experiment. Ultimately, whatever you choose will be delicious.

These brownies are best if slightly undercooked, so they still retain their gooeyness. What you want is a brownie that gets stuck to your teeth when eating it.

200g unsalted butter, cubed

200g dark chocolate, chopped

3 large eggs

275g caster sugar

90g plain flour

50g cocoa powder

250–300g ingredients of your choice to add to the mix (white, dark or milk chocolate, chocolate biscuits, your favourite chocolate bar), chopped

Makes 9–18 (depending on levels of greediness)

Preheat the oven to 190°C/170°C fan/gas 5. Line a 23cm square baking tin with baking parchment.

Put the butter and chocolate into a heatproof bowl over a pan of barely simmering water and leave until they start to melt. Stir regularly, taking care not to burn the chocolate. Once completely melted, remove from the heat and leave to cool a little.

In a large bowl, using an electric whisk on high power, beat the eggs and sugar together until pale and almost doubled in volume. Add the cooled chocolate and butter mix and gently combine, using a figure-of-eight motion to fold the 2 mixtures into one another.

Sift the flour and cocoa powder together and then fold into the chocolate and egg mixture. Again, fold gently using a figure-of-eight motion until all is combined. It will appear dusty at first, but be patient and it will come together. Take care not to overdo the mixing: as soon as you cannot see any dusty flour mix, you are there.

Now add your extra ingredients and gently fold in, reserving a few to scatter over the top if you like. Transfer the mixture to the lined baking tin, levelling it out and pressing any reserved ingredients into the top of the mixture. Bake for around 35 minutes. The top should be just firm, but the middle should be slightly undercooked and gooey: it will continue to cook in the tin once removed from the oven. Leave the tin on a wire rack to cool before cutting into squares.

Blackberry and Custard Tart

Jessie

Thank goodness for Clara, my old friend – and a professional chef – for helping us with this creation. A queen of sweet and pretty dishes, Clara thought Nigella Lawson would appreciate this and kindly offered up the recipe. We use a block of ready-made sweet pastry, but make your own if you dare.

My brother Alex, being Alex (and far more professional than Mum or I), made two tarts. One tart I ate before the Goddess arrived and the second I enjoyed even more, perversely watching her eat every mouthful. This is a gorgeous tart that perfectly balances sweet and sharp. It's just as good with raspberries instead of blackberries. This can be made a day in advance and chilled overnight. We like to serve this with crème fraîche.

plain flour, for dusting

500g sweet shortcrust pastry

4 large egg yolks

125g golden caster sugar

300ml double cream

2 tsp vanilla extract or, for added depth, the seeds scraped from 1 vanilla pod

pinch of salt

250g of the sweetest, juiciest blackberries you can find

icing sugar, to serve (optional)

Serves 8

Preheat the oven to 200°C/180°C fan/gas 6.

On a lightly floured surface, roll out the pastry to about 3mm thick, then use to line a 23cm loose-bottomed tart tin (about 3.5cm deep). Trim off any excess pastry from around the edges, then line with a large circle of baking parchment (scrunch it up first, then open it out so it's easier to mould into the case). Fill with baking beans or rice, then blind bake the pastry case for 20 minutes.

Carefully remove the parchment and beans and bake for another 5 minutes until the pastry is cooked through.

In a large bowl, combine the egg yolks, sugar, cream, vanilla and pinch of salt, and vigorously whisk until frothy and smooth.

Turn the oven down to 180°C/160°C fan/gas 4. Arrange the blackberries in the pastry case. Pour over the egg yolk mix and bake for around 30–40 minutes until the top is lightly golden (if it is colouring too quickly, cover loosely with a piece of foil) and still has a slight wobble in the centre.

Leave the tin on a wire rack to cool completely. If you like, dust with a little icing sugar just before serving.

Lemon and Elderflower Mascarpone Cupcakes

Jessie   We all got the lemon/elderflower memo when Meghan and Harry used my local – and fantastic – Violet Cakes to create their lemon and elderflower wedding cake.

Here is my brother Alex's interpretation and gift of a cupcake. As the frosting of these divine bites contains mascarpone, it's best to put the cupcakes in the fridge until just before you are ready to eat them (otherwise they may become a little sweaty and melted). Ideally eat on the day of making, or they can be kept in the fridge for a couple of days.

225g unsalted butter, softened

225g caster sugar

4 large eggs

3 tbsp elderflower cordial

grated zest of 1 lemon, plus juice of ½ lemon

225g self-raising flour

pinch of salt

MASCARPONE ICING

250g mascarpone cheese

2 tbsp icing sugar

3½ tbsp elderflower cordial

zest of 1 lemon, removed using a lemon zester

Makes around 12 cupcakes

Preheat the oven to 200°C/180°C fan/gas 6. Line a cupcake tin with paper cupcake cases.

In a large bowl, beat together the butter and sugar until pale and creamy. Next, add the eggs, elderflower cordial and lemon zest and juice, and whisk well until completely combined. The mixture will separate and look like it is curdling, but don't panic.

Sift in the flour and salt and fold until all is well combined and you have a thick mixture. Divide the mix among the cupcake cases, leaving a little room at the top of each case to allow the cupcakes to rise.

Bake on the middle shelf of the oven for 12–15 minutes. Keep an eye on your cupcakes – they are ready when they are golden brown and no longer wobbly in the middle but still retaining a little bounce when lightly pressed. Remove from the oven and leave to cool completely.

While the cupcakes are cooling, make your icing. Put the mascarpone in a bowl with the icing sugar and elderflower cordial and whisk well until completely combined. Put the bowl in the freezer for 20 minutes or in the fridge for an hour: this will thicken the icing and make it more manageable when icing your cakes.

When you are ready to ice the cakes, remove the icing from the fridge or freezer and give it another good mix. Pipe onto the cupcakes and finish with a couple of thin ribbons of lemon zest.

Banana Bread

Lennie My son Alex makes this all the time and even takes it to work when he's on night duty. It's a good way to use up slightly overripe bananas. We have served it on its own, toasted with butter and cinnamon, or with ice cream to guests on the podcast. It always goes down a treat.

Jessie I rather like this toasted with peanut butter, which Mum finds a little strange.

280g plain flour

1 tsp bicarbonate of soda

pinch of salt

110g unsalted butter at room temperature, plus extra for greasing

220g caster sugar

4 very ripe bananas

2 large eggs

80ml milk, mixed with the juice of ½ lemon

1 tsp vanilla extract

100g bar of dark chocolate (or milk if you prefer)

Serves 8

Preheat the oven to 200°C/180°C fan/gas 6. Butter and line a 1.5-litre loaf tin.

Sift the flour, bicarbonate of soda and salt into a large mixing bowl.

In a separate bowl, cream the softened butter and sugar together using an electric whisk, or persevere by hand, until pale and fluffy.

Give the bananas a good mash, using a potato masher, but don't worry if there are some larger banana pieces – this will give the loaf character. Add to the butter and sugar and stir to mix. Now add the eggs, milk and vanilla and mix well.

Next, fold the flour into the banana mix, using a metal spoon in a figure-of-eight motion. Combine well until there is no dusty flour left.

Take the bar of chocolate, still in its packet, and give it a few good whacks against the corner of your kitchen worktop, alternating the side of the packet so that all the chocolate gets broken up. Open the packet and if the demolished pieces still look too chunky, break up a little more using a sharp knife. However, in this case size does matter and you want nice big bits of chocolate for your loaf.

Add the chocolate to the banana mix, combine well and transfer to your lined loaf tin. Bake for about 45–55 minutes until risen and golden. Using a knife or a skewer, test the centre of the loaf: it should still be reasonably moist and gooey (but not dripping away from your knife/ skewer). Do not overcook or the loaf will be dry. Remove from the oven and leave to cool before slicing and serving.

Tip If you like, replace half the caster sugar with light brown sugar, which will give it a more caramel flavour.

Index

A

Alex's orange pistachio cake 262–5
anchovies
· anchovy dressing 59
· Jansson's temptation 211
· salsa verde 111
apples
· currant and apple coleslaw 143
· spiced red cabbage 221
· Stilton, red onion, apple and walnut tart 208
apricots
· apricot and walnut stuffing 212
· chicken with apricots 138
· Marbella chicken 100
artichokes: hot artichoke and spinach dip 27
asparagus
· asparagus with anchovy dressing 59
· griddled asparagus with pistachios and Cheddar 166
· primavera risotto 40
aubergine and Puy lentil Bolognese 82

B

Babybel bifteki burgers 180
bake, courgette 67
banana bread 278
basil: salsa verde 111
beans
· Bella's cod in sherry with roasted tomatoes and butter beans 112–13
· butter bean hummus 27
· sausage and bean casserole 85
beef
· Babybel bifteki burgers 180
· beef stifado 179
· beef tagliata 50
· brisket in cola 144
· Dave's devotional Thai beef salad 88
· meat stuffing 212
· rare onglet steak 86
· rare roast beef salad 163
· roast beef and Yorkshires 226
· salt beef 140
· sticky short ribs 93
beetroot
· beetroot and gin-cured salmon 198
· beetroot, watercress and hazelnut salad with horseradish dressing 75
Bella's cod in sherry with roasted tomatoes and butter beans 112–13
Benny's drunken croûton and kale salad 32
bifteki burgers, Babybel 180
blackberry and custard tart 275

blinis with horseradish cream and smoked salmon 205
Bolognese, aubergine and Puy lentil 82
Boursin: roasted Boursin chicken and leeks 47
bouyiourdi eggs 154
bread
· apricot and walnut stuffing 212
· Benny's drunken croûton and kale salad 32
· bread sauce 217
· meatballs with ouzo 174
· pitta chips 28
bread and butter pudding, panettone 259
Brie and cranberry parcels 201
brisket in cola 144
brownies, 'triple thread' chocolate 270
Brussels sprouts: roasted Brussels sprouts with grapes and hazelnuts 218
buffalo wings, Kitty's 103
burgers, Babybel bifteki 180
butter beans
· Bella's cod in sherry with roasted tomatoes and butter beans 112–13
· butter bean hummus 27
· sausage and bean casserole 85
butter-poached roast potatoes 99
butternut squash: roasted butternut squash with pink peppercorns 56

C

cabbage
· currant and apple coleslaw 143
· spiced red cabbage 221
cakes
· Alex's orange pistachio cake 262–5
· banana bread 278
· chocolate courgette cake 266
· 'triple threat' chocolate brownies 270
capers
· anchovy dressing 59
· fava dip 190
· Marbella chicken 100
cappuccino: no-churn cappuccino ice cream 254
carrots
· chick in a brick 107
· chicken soup 132
· currant and apple coleslaw 143
· Marmite carrot soup 38
· Mum's leftover turkey casserole 225
· roasted pickled carrot salad with ricotta and rocket 159
cashews: Nora's mushroom and cashew curry 80
casseroles
· Mum's leftover turkey casserole 225
· sausage and bean casserole 85

caviar, pasta with smoked salmon, vodka and 62
celeriac and potato gratin 53
celery
· Kitty's buffalo wings 103
· roasted Boursin chicken and leeks 47
cheese
· Babybel bifteki burgers 180
· Benny's drunken croûton and kale salad 32
· blue cheese dip 103
· bouyiourdi eggs 154
· Brie and cranberry parcels 201
· celeriac and potato gratin 53
· courgette bake 67
· easy-peasy chicken or turkey schnitzel 137
· Gorgonzola, fig and walnut tartlets 200
· griddled asparagus with pistachios and Cheddar 166
· griddled baby leeks with feta 167
· hot artichoke and spinach dip 27
· labneh 186–9
· Lennie's Puy lentil salad 158
· onion quiche 35
· Parmesan and spring onion mash 55
· rare roast beef salad 163
· savoury cheesecake 79
· spanakopita 164
· spicy lamb in filo 170–3
· Stilton, red onion, apple and walnut tart 208
· Toft sausage rolls 43
· see also mascarpone cheese; ricotta
cheesecake, savoury 79
cherries: Vera Sequira's chocolate and rum pudding 251
chicken
· chick in a brick 107
· chicken paillard 182
· chicken soup 132
· chicken with apricots 138
· easy-peasy chicken schnitzel 137
· Kitty's buffalo wings 103
· Marbella chicken 100
· Provençal roast chicken with olive tapenade 48
· roasted Boursin chicken and leeks 47
chicken livers
· Lennie's Friday night chopped liver 128
· quick and easy chicken liver pâté 207
chocolate
· banana bread 278
· chocolate courgette cake 266
· chocolate mousse tart 236
· chocolate soured cream ganache 266
· 'triple threat' chocolate brownies 270
· Vera Sequira's chocolate and rum pudding 251
coconut: Jessie's granola 22

Acknowledgements

Jessie

There are so many people to thank for helping to make this book.

Mum – I'm sorry I ever fooled you into thinking a podcast was just you making a couple of meals and meeting some of my mates. Thank you for being the star and the crux of this book's inspiration and soul. I love you – you are brilliant. And I promise to tidy up more in the kitchen.

Thank you to Alex for always being able to rustle up a pud and being so good at it.

To our wonderful agent Charlie, who has always embraced the madness and loudness of the Wares and been so incredibly generous with ideas and enthusiasm.

To the brilliant editorial team at Ebury: Lizzy, Emily and Maggie. Thank you for helping us create a book that we are so proud of, for all your wisdom and direction, and for your patience!

Thanks to our recipe testers, Eleanor, Samantha and Myles, and to the shoot team, Tamara, Ola, Wei, Sophie and Barbara, for bringing our recipes to life so beautifully.

To Ollie, for capturing the spirit of us and being a dream to work with.

To Sandra, for putting together a gorgeous book.

Thank you to our amazing management team Peter and Sarah – we could never do it without you; to Becky for setting the wheels in motion; and to Alice, who not only produces us but also contributes recipes and laughter.

Thank you to all our friends who have lent some of our favourite recipes.

Lastly, thank you to all the wonderful guests we have cooked for – our conversations have been so important to how we shaped this book.

Lennie

Firstly, thank you to all our wonderful guests on *Table Manners*, who inspired the cooking, the recipes and the cookbook.

Thanks to all our family and friends who have contributed the odd recipe, and particularly to Alexander Ware, who has concocted and cooked fabulous recipes, worked as soux-chef to us, made desserts and baked cakes, all when he is not busy saving lives (did I mention he is a doctor?!).

Thank you to Charlie Brotherstone, our fabulous agent, who has been such a support and great fun.

Thank you to Becky, who helped establish *Table Manners*.

Big thank you to Fascination Management for their unswerving support and sense of humour, often intervening in the odd mother-and-daughter dispute.

Thanks to Alice, our producer on *Table Manners*, for her professionalism and for being such good fun, as well as helping with the cooking from time to time.

Thanks to the editorial team at Ebury: Lizzy, Emily and Maggie. To Ola for her wonderful photographs and to her assistant Barbara. To Tamara and her assistant Sophie for making our food look delicious. And to Wei for inspirational props and styling.

Finally, the biggest thank you to my darling Jessie, who has always enjoyed my cooking, taught me about podcasts, and encouraged me to cook for people I never thought I'd meet in my wildest dreams. I've learned so much and hope that being bossy in the kitchen has not been too annoying. I think together we have created a cookbook that embraces our family, culture and love of entertaining.

10 9 8 7 6 5 4

Ebury Press, an imprint of
Ebury Publishing,
20 Vauxhall Bridge Road, London,
SW1V 2SA

Ebury Press is part of the Penguin Random House
group of companies whose addresses can be found
at global.penguinrandomhouse.com

First published by Ebury Press in 2020

www.penguin.co.uk

A CIP catalogue record for this book is available
from the British Library

Publishing director: Lizzy Gray
Project editor: Emily Preece-Morrison
Designer: Sandra Zellmer
Food photographer: Ola O. Smit
Cover photography and
pages 3, 6, 7, 141 and 235: Ollie Grove
Food stylist: Tamara Vos
Prop stylist: Wei Tang
Copy editor: Maggie Ramsay

ISBN: 9781529105209

Colour origination by Alta Image
Printed and bound in Italy by L.E.G.O. S.p.A